Perfectly LOGICAL!

CHALLENGING FUN BRAIN TEASERS AND LOGIC PUZZLES FOR SMART KIDS

JENN LARSON

ROCKRIDGE
PRESS

Written by Jenn Larsen

Designed by Creative Giant Inc., Mike Thomas, Chris Dickey, and Paul Tutrone.

Editor: Lia Brown

Photo credits: Creative Giant Inc, Discott, Ashlyak at ml.wikipedia, Dominik Stodulski, André Karwath aka Aka, Patrick Giraud, Mukul2u, Nicolás García, Charles J Sharp, Alan Cleaver, Martin Falbisoner, Diego Delso, Tage Olsin, aussiegall from sydney, Australia, COD Newsroom, Ken Thomas, MarkBuckawicki, Carlos Estrada, Bengt Oberger, Pogrebnoj-Alexandroff, Amgauna, Mokkie, S Sepp, Anna Anichkova, Anne Toal, Kevin.Sebold, stef yau, Miya, I, Luc Viatour, Abhijit Tembhekar from Mumbai, India, Alexandre Buisse (Nattfodd), Sepht, David Earle, Miroslav Duchacek (from Czech Republic), PanBK at the English language Wikipedia, D J Shin, Dale Cruse, Jennifer C., Cezary p, dronepicr, Debasish biswas kolkata, Crisdip, Pixabay, Carlos Delgado, Edwin Torres from USA, Andy Morffew

ISBN: 978-1-64152-531-2

CONTENTS

Ever since I was little, I've enjoyed solving puzzles and brain teasers. I love the satisfaction you get when you start with a blank puzzle, ready to be solved, and end up with a completed crossword puzzle or a tough Sudoku! Now, as a teacher for more than 20 years, logic puzzles and brain teasers still capture my attention. They're a great way for kids to exercise their brains while having fun!

In fact, logic puzzles and brain teasers provide so many benefits:

- Improve problem-solving skills
- Strengthen visual-spatial reasoning
- Enhance memory and processing speed
- Increase abstract thinking skills
- Improve concentration and attention span
- Lift mood, lower stress and anxiety
- Help develop patience and determination
- Increase self-confidence and provide a sense of accomplishment

In this book, you'll find a wide variety of fun logic puzzles and brain teasers: pattern recognition, analogies, code breakers, logic grid puzzles, crossword puzzles, rebus puzzles, Sudoku and Mathdoku, cryptograms, matchstick puzzles, and odd one out.

Each type of puzzle or brain teaser targets a slightly different set of reasoning skills, helping the problem solver become a well-rounded logical thinker! Some puzzles focus on images and patterns, some puzzles focus on math concepts, while other puzzles focus on vocabulary and connections between words. Regardless of the type, it's my hope that these puzzles will not only exercise the brain, but provide lots of fun for the problem solver!

Each chapter consists of nine puzzles that start out simple but become more challenging as the chapter moves along. The last puzzle in each chapter is called a Brain Bender. This is the most challenging puzzle and may have additional hints included.

The answers to the puzzles can be found at the back of the book. Keep in mind that for some of the more creative puzzles it is impossible to list every alternative answer. If the problem solver thinks outside of the box, he/she may think of additional answers that are equally correct and should be accepted.

There are a number of ways to use this book. Problem solvers can work chapter to chapter from start to end without stopping! Some kids may want to do all the simpler puzzles from each chapter first, saving the medium and more difficult puzzles for later. Another alternative is to skip around and complete any puzzle. There really is no right or wrong way to use the book! The most important thing is for kids to have fun, while using logical reasoning.

Logical thinking weighs important facts and ideas in a sequential way to create conclusions. This type of thinking is a critical component of math reasoning but is helpful in all areas. The good news is that logical thinking is not static and may be improved with practice! Using logic puzzles and brain teasers helps learners think sequentially and develop and test hypotheses to improve their logical thinking skills.

Each chapter provides different learning experiences and may be used in a number of ways. In the classroom, the puzzles may be used for early finishers, enrichment, and literacy or math centers. Parents or homeschool teachers may also use the puzzles for enrichment, as part of a language or math curriculum, or for travel. The best part of these logic puzzles and brain teasers is that they provide beneficial brain exercise in a fun way that doesn't feel like work!

CHAPTER 1: PATTERNS AT PLAY (Pattern Recognition)

This chapter includes patterns using shapes, numbers, and matrices. The ability to recognize patterns and extend them is important not only for mathematical thinking, but also for music, art, science, and literature. Identifying patterns is beneficial as it activates both sides of the brain. This type of puzzle encourages problem solvers to understand the relationships between objects and test hypotheses to make generalizations.

CHAPTER 2: FOLLOW THAT ANALOGY (Analogies)

A variety of analogy types are presented in this chapter, from words to shapes and math analogies. By analyzing language and numerical relationships, problem solvers build connections between old and new learning. This careful analysis of how things are related is a learning strategy that extends to all subjects. An added benefit of practicing analogies is that they often appear on many assessments and ability tests.

CHAPTER 3: MISSION CODE BREAKERS (Shapes and Pictures)

This chapter is filled with different code breakers that help with deductive reasoning practice. These brain teasers require the problem solver to organize information that may seem unrelated, and to form and test hypotheses. Knowledge of language, vocabulary, and spelling also plays a part in the successful completion of the puzzles.

CHAPTER 4: SIMPLY LOGICAL (Logic Grid Puzzles)

The logic puzzles in this chapter range from a single grid to multiple grids. This type of mental exercise activates the vertical thinking, analytical left side of the brain. Learning to use a step-by-step method is a beneficial strategy. Although logic puzzles may seem more like a mental exercise than a mathematical one, these puzzles demonstrate both functions and relations, which are key mathematical concepts.

CHAPTER 5: CROSSWORDS TO CONSIDER (Crossword Puzzles)

This chapter offers a variety of crossword puzzles with high-interest topics. Crossword puzzles provide valuable spelling practice and allow learners to differentiate between similar words. This type of puzzle helps students learn and reinforce vocabulary words, increasing their knowledge of language. Besides concrete language skills, crossword puzzles promote higher-level thinking strategies like making inferences and drawing conclusions.

CHAPTER 6: WHIMSICAL WORDS (Rebus Puzzles)

The rebus puzzles in this chapter use word position, symbols, and numbers to represent common phrases. Students combine visual clues with their knowledge of word patterns and language to decipher a puzzle's meaning. While the puzzles exercise both sides of the brain, they are particularly good at encouraging lateral thinking, which is thinking creatively or outside of the box.

CHAPTER 7: MINDFUL MATH (Sudoku and Mathdoku)

This chapter has Sudoku and Mathdoku puzzles which ask learners to identify number patterns and use critical thinking in order to solve the puzzles successfully. Using decision-making skills as well as logical deductions are an integral part of these types of games. Since problem solvers must play close attention to details, Sudoku and Mathdoku also result in improved concentration.

CHAPTER 8: CURIOUS CRYPTOGRAMS (Cryptograms)

The cryptograms in this chapter are kid-friendly but still challenging! Cryptograms are word puzzles with spaces for letters. Problem solvers have to decipher the code to figure out which letter matches which number using analytical thinking. This type of game activates the left side of the brain since knowledge of language and word patterns is required in order to complete the puzzles.

CHAPTER 9: MIND YOUR MATCHSTICKS (Matchstick Puzzles)

In this chapter, problem solvers must move matchsticks (or toothpicks, cotton swabs, or pieces of paper) to create new shapes or to correctly solve math problems. The puzzles are a good way to exercise different parts of the brain using careful observation, visual-spatial imagery, and abstract thinking. They also require trial and error and persistence to find solutions.

CHAPTER 10: ODD BIRDS (Odd One Out)

Odd one out puzzles present several different objects or groups of objects and ask which one does not belong. These visual discrimination puzzles encourage deductive reasoning. Problem solvers practice recognizing the common attributes of objects, creating rules for that information, and then generating a conclusion based on observations. The puzzles help improve visual perception skills used every day.

CHAPTER 1

PATTERNS AT PLAY

Whether it's a honeycomb, the bricks on a building, or rows of corn, you've probably noticed patterns in the world around you.

This chapter is all about patterns, and you'll find a variety of pattern puzzles to solve. Some have shapes, some have numbers, while others are on a matrix. As the chapter moves along, the puzzles will get more challenging!

SHAPE MYSTERIES

NAME: _____

Look at each pattern below. Which two shapes come next?

1. ▢ △ △ △ ● ● ● ▢ △ ____ ____

2. ➡ ⬇ ⬅ ⬆ ➡ ____ ____

3. ★ ★ ◆ ◆ ▽ ▽ ★ ____ ____

4. ▭ ⬭ ● ♥ ⬯ ▭ ⬭ ____ ____

5. ▲ ▼ ⬠ ⬠ ⬆ ⬇ ⬯ ____ ____

SHAPE FACT:

THE BERMUDA TRIANGLE IS AN AREA OF THE ATLANTIC OCEAN WHERE PLANES AND BOATS HAVE MYSTERIOUSLY DISAPPEARED! THE AREA COVERS 500,000 SQUARE MILES AND IS LOCATED BETWEEN FLORIDA, PUERTO RICO, AND BERMUDA.

ANSWERS ON PAGE 101

NAME: _____

A matrix is a grid with rows and columns. Look at the pattern in the matrix.
Find the square that would best complete the matrix. Circle it.

1.

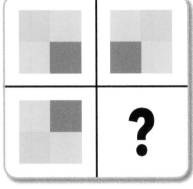   

2.

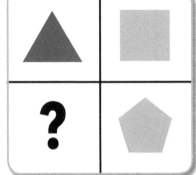   

3.

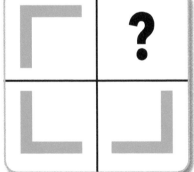   

MAGICIAN FACT:

HARRY HOUDINI WAS ONE OF THE MOST FAMOUS MAGICIANS OF ALL TIME! ONE OF HIS MOST POPULAR TRICKS WAS FIRST SEEN IN NEW YORK CITY IN 1918. IT WAS CALLED THE VANISHING ELEPHANT!

BUZZING ABOUT NUMBERS

NAME: _____

Look at each pattern below. Which two numbers come next?

1. | 5 | 10 | 15 | 20 | 25 | 30 | 35 | 40 | | |

2. | 1 | 2 | 2 | 3 | 3 | 3 | 4 | 4 | | |

3. | 90 | 9 | 80 | 8 | 70 | 7 | 60 | 6 | | |

4. | 11 | 22 | 33 | 44 | 55 | 66 | 77 | 88 | | |

5. | 1 | 2 | 4 | 8 | 16 | 32 | 64 | 128 | | |

6. | 3 | 4 | 6 | 9 | 13 | 18 | 24 | 31 | | |

ANSWERS ON PAGE 101

NAME: _____

Look at the patterns made on the dots. Copy each pattern.

1.

2.

3.
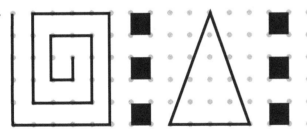

4.
 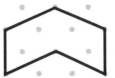

BIG CAT FACT:

WHAT'S AN EASY WAY TO TELL THE DIFFERENCE BETWEEN
CHEETAHS AND LEOPARDS? CHEETAHS ARE COVERED IN
LOTS OF SINGLE BLACK SPOTS, WHILE LEOPARDS HAVE
SPOTS THAT ARE GROUPED TOGETHER CALLED ROSETTES!

PICTURE-CHANGING PATTERNS

NAME: _____

Look at the shapes in the first box. Think about how the first shape changed to become the second one. Look at the shapes in the next box. Circle the shape that shows how the first shape in that box would change if it followed a similar pattern.

ANSWERS ON PAGE 101

SPOT THE METAMORPHOSIS!

NAME: _____

Look at the shapes in the first box. Think about how the first shape changed to become the second one. Look at the shapes in the next box. Circle the shape that shows how the first shape in that box would change if it followed a similar pattern.

MARVELOUS MATRICES

NAME: _____

Which square best completes each matrix? Circle it.

1.

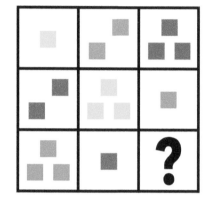

2.

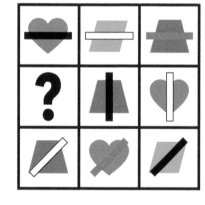

3.

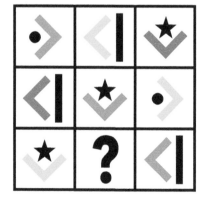

NAME: _____

Which square best completes each matrix? Circle it.

1.

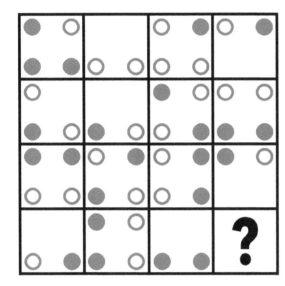

2.

CLOCK FACT:

IN LONDON, ENGLAND, YOU CAN SEE BIG BEN, WHICH IS THE BIGGEST FOUR-FACED, CHIMING CLOCK IN THE WORLD! TO SET BIG BEN'S HANDS BACKWARD OR FORWARD IN THE FALL OR SPRING TAKES 16 HOURS!

ANSWERS ON PAGE 102   **9**

NAME: _____

Find the puzzle piece that completes the pattern.

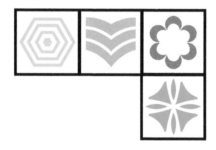

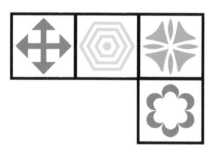

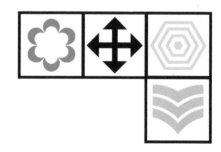

ANSWERS ON PAGE 102

CHAPTER 2

FOLLOW THAT ANALOGY

Analogies are all about relationships. That means figuring out how two things are related and then using that information to find another set of ideas that are related in the same way.

In this chapter, you'll find word analogies, number analogies, and picture analogies too. Don't forget . . . the puzzles will get more challenging as you move along!

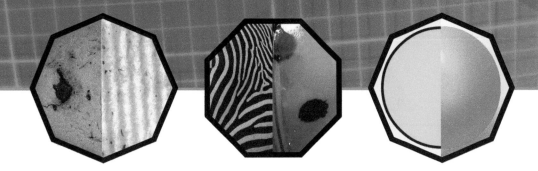

SHAPE UP ANALOGIES

NAME: _____

Draw the shape that best completes the analogy.

1. ⬤ : ⊗ :: ⬛ :

2. ⬜ : 4 :: ⬠ :

3. ◆ : ⧖ :: ⊖ :

4. ◎ : ● :: ⬜ :

5. △ : △(dots) :: ◇ :

6. ◣ : ◭ :: ▯ :

7. ⬡ : ⬡ :: ✕ :

8. ⇨ : ⇦ :: ▷ :

ANSWERS ON PAGE 102

SPORTS ANALOGIES

NAME: _____

Write the word that best completes the analogy.

1. **RACQUET** is to **TENNIS** as **BAT** is to _____

2. **PING PONG BALL** is to **LIGHT** as **BOWLING BALL** is to _____

3. **BASKETBALL** is to **REFEREE** as **BASEBALL** is to _____

4. **SNOW SKIING** is to **TWO** as **SNOWBOARDING** is to _____

5. **ICE SKATES** is to **BLADES** as **ROLLER SKATES** is to _____

6. **HOCKEY** is to **RINK** as **BASKETBALL** is to _____

7. **SKATEBOARD** is to **FOUR** as **SURFBOARD** is to _____

8. **TOUCHDOWN** is to **FOOTBALL** as **GOAL** is to _____

9. **PARACHUTING** is to **AIR** as **SAILING** is to _____

10. **SUMO WRESTLER** is to **BIG** as **JOCKEY** is to _____

11. **RUNNING** is to **TRACK** as **SWIMMING** is to _____

12. **SPRINT** is to **SHORT** as **MARATHON** is to _____

BASEBALL FACT:

ABOUT 20 MILLION HOT DOGS
ARE SERVED AT MAJOR LEAGUE
BASEBALL GAMES EACH YEAR!

YUMMY ANALOGIES

NAME: _____

Circle the picture that best completes the analogy.

1. **SWEET** is to **CUPCAKE**   as   **SALTY** is to

2. **VINE** is to **GRAPES**   as   **TREE** is to

3. **HOT** is to **SOUP**   as   **COLD** is to

4. **PIT** is to **PEACH**   as   **SEED** is to

5. **CARNIVAL** is to **COTTON CANDY**   as   **MOVIES** is to

6. **CUT** is to **KNIFE**   as   **STIR** is to

7. **CIRCLE** is to **WHOLE PIZZA**   as   **SECTOR** is to

8. **FORK** is to **SALAD**   as   **HAND** is to

CUPCAKE FACT:

THE WORLD'S LARGEST CUPCAKE WEIGHED OVER 1,200 LBS. AND WAS TOPPED WITH 600 LBS. OF FROSTING!

ANSWERS ON PAGE 102

ANIMAL ANALOGIES

NAME: _____

Write the word that best completes the analogy.

1. BEAR : CUB as CAT : _____

2. RABBIT : FUR as CROCODILE : _____

3. LION : ROAR as _____ : BARK

4. MONKEY : TROOP as WOLF : _____

5. CHEETAH : FAST as SLOTH : _____

6. TENTACLES : OCTOPUS as TRUNK : _____

7. BEAVER : DAM as ROBIN : _____

8. HORSE : GALLOP as KANGAROO : _____

9. GILLS : FISH as _____ : MAMMAL

10. ZEBRA : STRIPED as LADYBUG : _____

11. PENGUIN : SWIM as EAGLE : _____

12. DEER : FOREST as CAMEL : _____

13. PEACOCK : STRUT as SNAKE : _____

14. WHALE : ENORMOUS as ANT : _____

15. WISE : OWL as _____ : FOX

FRACTIONS AND LETTERS FUN!

NAME: _____

Draw the object that best completes the analogy.

1.	**F**	:	**E**	::	**I**	:
2.	△	:	▲	::	⬠	:
3.	**A**	:	**V**	::	**H**	:
4.	⊛	:	⊛	::	⬡	:
5.	**Z**	:	⧖	::	**K**	:
6.	⬡	:	⬡	::	△△	:
7.	**E**	:	E E E	::	**M**	:
8.	⊞	:	⊞	::	▦	:

POPCORN FACT:

AT 14 BILLION QUARTS A YEAR, MORE POPCORN IS EATEN IN THE UNITED STATES THAN IN ANY OTHER COUNTRY IN THE WORLD!

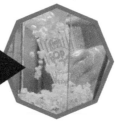

ANSWERS ON PAGE 103

ANALOGIES AT WORK!

NAME: _____

Circle the picture that best completes the analogy.

1. **CLIMB** is to **LADDER** as **CARRY** is to

2. **COOK** is to **CHEF** as **PAINT** is to

3. **ARCHITECT** is to **BUILDING** as **COMPOSER** is to

4. **HAMMER** is to **CARPENTER** as **TEST TUBE** is to

5. **COMB** is to **HAIR** as **RAKE** is to

6. **TEACHER** is to **CLASSROOM** as **ENGINEER** is to

7. **FASHION DESIGNER** is to **CLOTHES** as **AUTHOR** is to

8. **POLICE OFFICER** is to **BADGE** as **SERVER** is to

MAD ABOUT MATH ANALOGIES

NAME: _____

Fill in the blanks to complete each math analogy.

1. ADD : SUBTRACT as **MULTIPLY :** _____

2. **ONE FOURTH : HALF** as HALF : _____

3. 9:00 AM : 9:00 PM as **NOON :** _____

4. **15, 20, 25 : 5** as 24, 32, 40 : _____

5. OCTAGON : 8 as **DECAGON :** _____

6. **GALLONS : LIQUID CAPACITY** as INCHES : _____

7. CENTIMETER : 1 as **METER :** _____

8. **TRIANGLE : 180°** as SQUARE : _____

9. 10 : 100 and 11 : 121 as **12 :** _____

10. **QUARTS : 4** as PINTS : _____

11. 42, 49, 56 : 7 as **54, 63, 72 :** _____

12. **CIRCLE : 2D** as SPHERE : _____

13. ACUTE, OBTUSE, RIGHT : ANGLES as
    SCALENE, EQUILATERAL, ISOSCELES : _____

14. **EVEN : 2, 4, 6, 8** as ODD : _____

15. CYLINDER : 3 as **CUBE :** _____

ANSWERS ON PAGE 103

ANALOGIES IN THE MIX!

NAME: _____

Complete the analogies by drawing, writing, or circling the answer.

1. FURRY is to **RACCOON** as **SPIKY** is to _____

2. **SUMO WRESTLING** is to **JAPAN** as **BASKETBALL** is to

3. 12 is to **FEET** as **36** is to _____

4. :

5. **MAMMAL** is to **MONKEY** as **AMPHIBIAN** is to

6. **SHAKING** is to **EARTHQUAKE** as **SPINNING** is to _____

7. **16 TBSP** is to **1 CUP** as **16 CUPS** is to _____

8.

RACCOON FACT:

RACCOONS USE UP TO 200 DIFFERENT SOUNDS TO COMMUNICATE! THEY PURR, WHISTLE, CHITTER, GROWL, SCREAM, HISS, SCREECH, AND EVEN MAKE A SOUND SIMILAR TO A HORSE'S WHINNY.

BRAIN BENDER

Look at the analogies carefully! At first glance, many of the answers seem correct. Make sure to consider the relationship between the first set of words before choosing an answer with a similar connection. Circle the letter of the set of words that best completes the analogy.

1. EAGLE : TALON ::
   A. ELEPHANT : TRUNK
   B. LION : MANE
   C. SNAKE : FANGS

2. ENTERTAINING : AMUSING ::
   A. TEDIOUS : MONOTONOUS
   B. PUMA : CAT
   C. AMBIGUOUS : CLEAR

3. PROUD : STRUT ::
   A. BOASTFUL : JOG
   B. FURIOUS : ANGRY
   C. FURTIVE : TIPTOE

4. THYME : HERB ::
   A. POODLE : GOLDEN RETRIEVER
   B. SALMON : FISH
   C. WHALE : POD

5. CRUCIAL : TRIVIAL ::
   A. FASCINATING : BORING
   B. VITAL : INDISPENSABLE
   C. IMAGINATION : MIND

6. EGYPT : PYRAMIDS ::
   A. HIMALAYAS : MOUNT EVEREST
   B. SOUTH AMERICA : BRAZIL
   C. PARIS : EIFFEL TOWER

7. UNHAPPINESS : MISERY ::
   A. NERVOUS : UNEASY
   B. CONTENT : ECSTATIC
   C. DEPRESSED : ELATED

8. ANTIQUATED : ANCIENT ::
   A. PRIMITIVE : MODERN
   B. TRUSTWORTHY : DECEITFUL
   C. WRITER : AUTHOR

9. WANE : MOON ::
   A. EBB : TIDE
   B. STAR : SHINE
   C. SUNRISE : SUN

10. COMPASS : EXPLORER ::
    A. GPS : PHONE
    B. STARS : SAILORS
    C. TELESCOPE : ASTRONOMER

ANSWERS ON PAGE 103

CHAPTER 3

MISSION CODE BREAKERS

Code breaker puzzles use logic to analyze ideas. By recognizing which information to keep, which information to discard, and how the information is related, you'll become an expert code breaker in no time!

This chapter is filled with lots of code breakers, from Morse code to binary code, pigpen codes, and more! As the chapter moves along, the puzzles will get more challenging. Ready to start cracking?

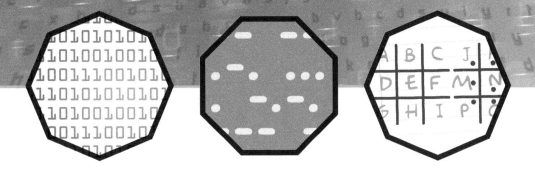

NAME: _____

Morse code is made of dots (shorter beeps) and dashes (longer beeps).
Use the Morse code chart to figure out the names of these famous paintings.

A •—	F ••—•	K —•—	P •——•	U ••—	Z ——••
B —•••	G ——•	L •—••	Q ——•—	V •••—	0 —————
C —•—•	H ••••	M ——	R •—•	W •——	1 •————
D —••	I ••	N —•	S •••	X —••—	2 ••———
E •	J •———	O ———	T —	Y —•——	3 •••——

1. ☐☐☐☐ ☐☐☐☐

—— ——— —• •— •—•• •• ••• •—

2. ☐☐☐ ☐☐☐☐☐☐

— •••• • ••• —•—• •—• • •— ——

3. ☐☐☐ ☐☐☐☐☐☐

•—• • —•• —••• •— •—•• •—•• ——— ——— •—

4. ☐☐☐☐☐☐☐☐☐☐☐ ☐☐☐☐

—•—• ——— —— •—• ——— ••• •• — •• ——— —• •••— •• •• ••

ANSWERS ON PAGE 104

NAME: _____

Each number represents a letter. Crack the code and fill in the grid
with ice cream flavors. Use the clues to get started!

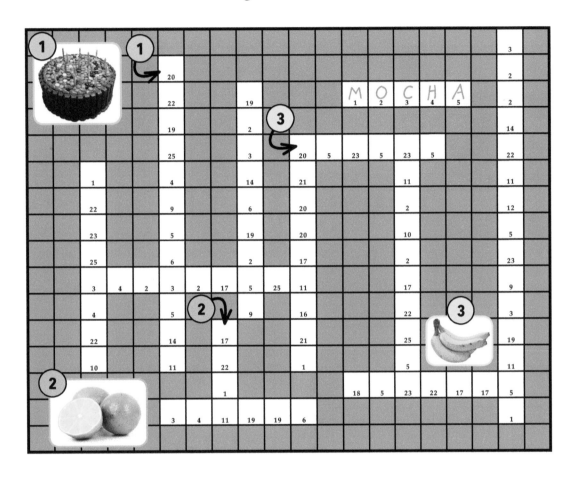

1	2	3	4	5	6	7	8	9	10	11	12	13
M	O	C	H	A			W					F

14	15	16	17	18	19	20	21	22	23	24	25	26
	Q									X		J

ICE CREAM FACT:

WAFFLE CONES BECAME POPULAR AT THE 1904 ST. LOUIS
WORLD'S FAIR! AN ICE CREAM STAND RAN OUT OF BOWLS,
SO THE WAFFLE SELLER IN THE NEXT STAND ROLLED UP A
THIN WAFFLE TO HOLD THE ICE CREAM!

BINARY CODE PICTURES

Computers and electronics use a binary system with only the numbers 0 and 1. The number 1 is "on" and 0 is "off." Color the pictures based on binary code. The first one is done for you!

10000001
11000011
11111111
11011011
11111111
11111111
10000001
11111111

10000001
01000010
00111100
00100100
00100100
00111100
01000010
10000001

Use the grid below to create your own binary picture. Make sure to add the binary code too!

ANSWERS ON PAGE 104

NAME: _____

Each number represents a letter. Crack the code and fill in the grid with game-related words. Use the clues to get started!

Code Tip: Don't decode this number four! It's part of the game title!

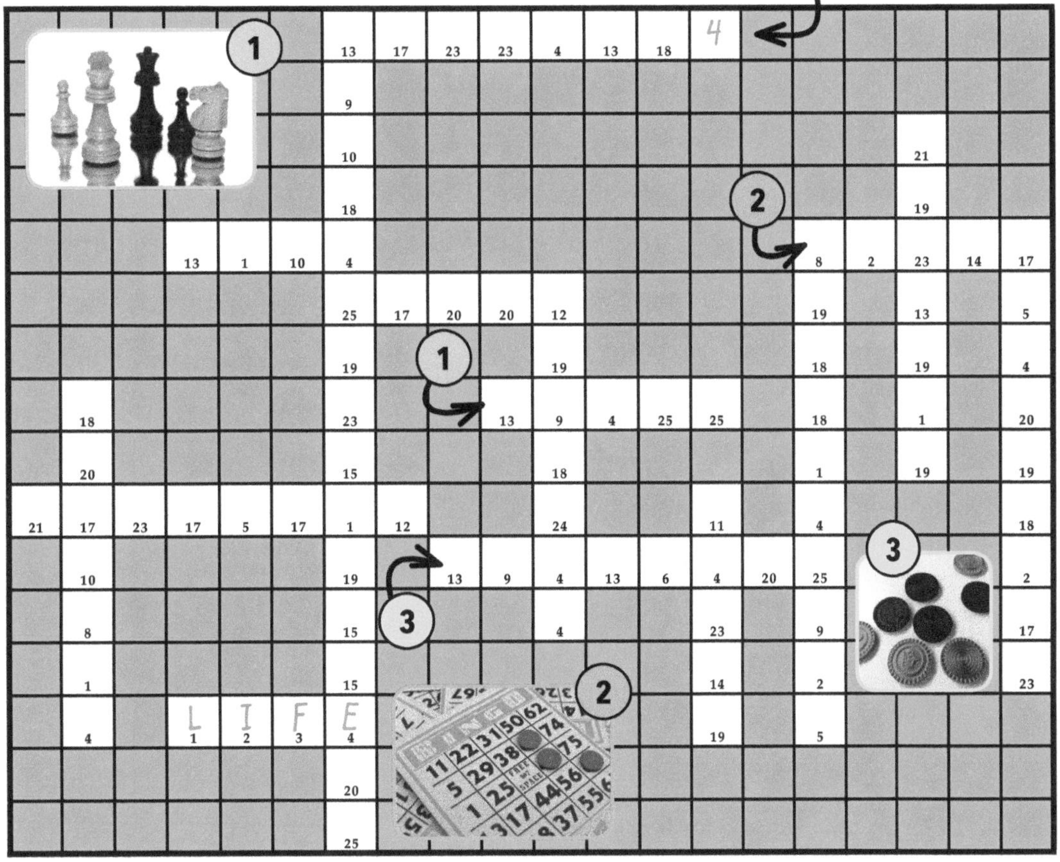

The grid contains numbered cells. Clue numbers 1, 2, 3 appear in circles pointing to entries.

Across/down entries include sequences such as:
13 17 23 23 4 13 18 4
8 2 23 14 17
25 17 20 20 12
23 13 9 4 25 25
21 17 23 17 5 17 1 12
19 13 9 4 13 6 4 20 25

L I F E (1 2 3 4)

Decode table:

1	2	3	4	5	6	7	8	9	10	11	12	13
L	I	F	E			W						

14	15	16	17	18	19	20	21	22	23	24	25	26
		X										Q

MONOPOLY FACT:

CHARLES DARROW CREATED THE MONOPOLY GAME IN 1933 IN HIS HOME. HE USED CLOTH FOR THE BOARD, HANDWRITTEN CARDS, AND WOODEN HOUSES AND HOTELS. HIS NIECES SUGGESTED GAME PIECES MADE OF METAL, LIKE THE SHAPES ON THEIR CHARM BRACELETS!

ANSWERS ON PAGE 104 **25**

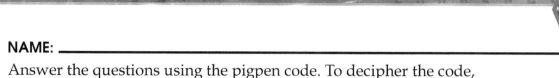

PIGPEN

NAME: _____

Answer the questions using the pigpen code. To decipher the code, look at the part of the "pigpen" that surrounds the letter.

For example: **A** = ⌐ , **L** = ⌐• , and **W** = ∨

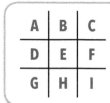

1. Pigs are the third most intelligent animals in the world after apes and _____.

   ___ ___ ___ ___ ___ ___ ___ ___

2. Pigs are related to which animals?

   ___ ___ ___ ___ ___ ___ ___ ___ ___

3. A pig's squeal can be very loud at 130 decibels. That's even louder than
   a _____ _____ at 120 decibels!

   ___ ___ ___ ___ ___ ___ ___ ___ ___

4. In _____, there are twice as many pigs as people.

   ___ ___ ___ ___ ___ ___ ___

26

ANSWERS ON PAGE 104

NAME: _____

Each number represents a letter. Crack the code and fill in the grid with objects related to outer space. Use the clues to get started!

1	2	3	4	5	6	7	8	9	10	11	12	13
M	A	R	S									
14	15	16	17	18	19	20	21	22	23	24	25	26
		K			Q	H			D	Z		W

SPACE FACT:

SCIENTISTS PLACED MESSAGES FOR POSSIBLE ALIENS ON THE VOYAGER 1 SPACE PROBE. THE MESSAGES CONTAIN GREETINGS FROM EARTH IN MANY LANGUAGES, AS WELL AS ANIMAL SOUNDS, SOUNDS OF NATURE, DIFFERENT KINDS OF MUSIC, AND LOTS OF IMAGES.

ANSWERS ON PAGE 105 **27**

CRACK THE CODE

Look at the code for the first four boxes. Use that information to figure out the code for the fifth box. Circle the letter under the correct answer.

1.

QA	RB	SC	RC	?

SB	RA	SA	QC
A	B	C	D

2.

LW	MX	NY	KW	?

LY	MY	NW	NV
A	B	C	D

3.

QD	HZ	SI	QZ	?

HD	HZ	QP	SZ
A	B	C	D

4.

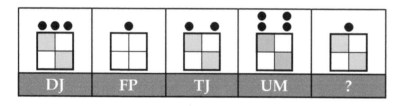

DJ	FP	TJ	UM	?

DP	UJ	FJ	TM
A	B	C	D

5.

ARS	NKT	LYB	AKB	?

AYS	LRB	NKB	LRS
A	B	C	D

ANSWERS ON PAGE 105

NAME: _____

Each number represents a letter. Crack the code and fill in the grid with objects related to the rainforest. Use the clues to get started!

1	2	3	4	5	6	7	8	9	10	11	12	13
S	L	O	T	H					W			

14	15	16	17	18	19	20	21	22	23	24	25	26
							X				Q	

SLOTH FACT:

SLOTHS SPEND MOST OF THEIR TIME IN TREES HANGING UPSIDE DOWN. SOMETIMES, THOUGH, THEY LIKE TO TAKE A SWIM. SLOTHS ARE EXCELLENT SWIMMERS AND DOGGY PADDLE THREE TIMES FASTER THAN THEY MOVE ON LAND!

ANSWERS ON PAGE 105 **29**

BRAIN BENDER

NAME: _____

You are a spy trying to obtain a top-secret document from a locked safe! Use the clues to figure out the three-digit passcode. Place each passcode in the blank boxes.

1.

6 4 5	One number is correct and in the right spot.
6 8 9	One number is correct but in the wrong spot.
8 1 7	Two numbers are correct but in the wrong spots.
9 2 3	Nothing is correct.
9 1 4	One number is correct but in the wrong spot.

2.

8 6 9	One number is correct and in the right spot.
4 8 2	One number is correct but in the wrong spot.
9 3 1	Two numbers are correct but in the wrong spots.
5 1 6	Nothing is correct.
5 6 3	One number is correct but in the wrong spot.

3.

5 8 2	One number is correct and in the right spot.
1 0 3	One number is correct but in the wrong spot.
6 1 9	Two numbers are correct but in the wrong spots.
8 3 7	Nothing is correct.
9 7 5	One number is correct but in the wrong spot.

4.

8 1 6	One number is correct and in the right spot.
3 5 2	One number is correct but in the wrong spot.
7 9 3	Two numbers are correct but in the wrong spots.
5 6 9	Nothing is correct.
1 7 0	One number is correct but in the wrong spot.

ANSWERS ON PAGE 105

CHAPTER 4

SIMPLY LOGICAL

Logic puzzles give you clues and make you think! You'll be eliminating false information, while keeping what's true. You'll also be taking notes with X's and O's on grids to help you find the correct answers.

In this chapter, you'll find lots of logic puzzles, from simple grids to very complex puzzles. At first glance, some of the puzzles may seem impossible, but with a little determination and a lot of logic, you'll solve them successfully!

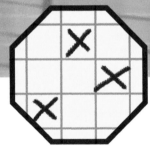

ALIEN LANDING

NAME: _____

Four aliens have landed on Earth! Your job is to use the clues to solve each logic puzzle to learn more about them. Use the grid to help you keep track of information! Draw an X in the boxes that can be eliminated and an O in the boxes that are a match. Each time you find an answer that is a match (O), cross out all choices vertically and horizontally in that category.

ALIEN AGES:

1. Nolp is the oldest alien.
2. Var's age is an odd number.
3. Azena has been alive for the same number of years as she has toes.

	AZENA	NOLP	ZEBLY	VAR
8				
9				
10				
11				

FAVORITE EARTH FOODS:

1. Zebly loves breakfast foods.
2. Var likes things that are sour.
3. Nolp has a sweet tooth.

	AZENA	NOLP	ZEBLY	VAR
PANCAKES				
JELLY BEANS				
PICKLES				
CORN DOGS				

ALIEN FACT:

IN 1947, A MAN IN ROSWELL, NEW MEXICO, FOUND FOIL REFLECTORS, METALLIC STICKS, AND OTHER STRANGE MATERIALS IN HIS SHEEP PASTURE. SOME PEOPLE WONDER IF THESE ITEMS WERE FROM AN ALIEN SPACESHIP!

ANSWERS ON PAGE 105

PICNIC TIME

NAME: _____

It's picnic time! Each friend is bringing an item to share, and the ants can't wait to dig in! Your job is to use the clues to solve each logic puzzle. You'll find out what each friend is bringing and how the ants plan to capture some of that food! Use the grid to keep track of information. Draw an X in the boxes that can be eliminated and an O in the boxes that are a match. Remember: Every time you find an answer that is a match (O), cross out all choices vertically and horizontally in that category.

PICNIC FOOD:

1. Jordan volunteered to bring the main dish.
2. Mariela wanted to bring something healthy to eat.
3. Ryan's mom suggested she refrigerate these overnight so they'd stay cold.

	HOT DOGS	CHIPS	FRUIT	DRINKS
MICHAEL				
MARIELA				
JORDAN				
RYAN				

PICNIC ANT STRATEGIES:

1. Antoinette is the fastest ant.
2. Antero is a red ant and blended in with the red tablecloth.
3. Antonia moved very quietly.

	DISTRACTION	CAMOUFLAGE	GRAB AND RUN	TIPTOE
ANTONIA				
ANTERO				
ANTOINETTE				
ANTONELLO				

ANT FACT:

ANTS ARE EXTREMELY STRONG AND CAN CARRY FROM 10 TO 50 TIMES THEIR BODY WEIGHT!

AT THE DONUT SHOP

NAME: _____

Use the clues and the grid to solve the puzzle. Draw an X in the boxes that can be eliminated and an O in the boxes that are a match. Remember: Every time you find an answer that is a match (O), cross out all choices vertically and horizontally in that category.

Four friends went to the donut shop for a special breakfast.
Each friend ordered a different donut and a different drink.

CLUES:

1. Jackson is allergic to chocolate but likes fruity drinks and fruity donuts.

2. Mia and Andrew like milk with their donuts, but Mia thinks whole milk is too rich and creamy.

3. The person who ordered the hot cocoa chose the apple fritter.

4. Neither Mia nor Andrew like jelly-filled donuts.

5. A girl ordered the maple donut.

	WHOLE MILK	NONFAT MILK	ORANGE JUICE	HOT COCOA	GLAZED TWIST	JELLY FILLED	MAPLE BAR	APPLE FRITTER
JACKSON								
MIA								
ANDREW								
LEE								
GLAZED TWIST								
JELLY FILLED								
MAPLE BAR								
APPLE FRITTER								

ANSWERS ON PAGE 106

PIRATE TREASURE

Use the clues and the grid to solve the puzzle. Draw an X in the boxes that can be eliminated and an O in the boxes that are a match. Each time you find an answer that is a match (O), cross out all choices vertically and horizontally in that category.

Four pirates in search of buried treasure landed on four deserted islands. Each of them had a treasure map leading to a different treasure. Use the clues to find out each pirate's nickname, as well as the treasure he/she found.

CLUES:

1. William and Charles did not find silver or jewels.

2. Maria, who lost her hand in a sword fight, did not find jewels.

3. The pirate who was called the Mad Captain found the gold coins. Charles found the gold.

4. The pirate who lost some toes to a hungry shark is a boy.

5. Isabel has an especially sparkly smile.

	SILVER TOOTH	MAD CAPTAIN	SHARP HOOK	JOLLY TWO TOES	GOLD	SILVER	JEWELS	GOLD COINS
MARIA								
WILLIAM								
ISABEL								
CHARLES								
GOLD								
SILVER								
JEWELS								
GOLD COINS								

PIRATE FACT:

PIRATES NEVER WHISTLED WHILE ON SHIP. IT WAS THOUGHT TO BRING BAD LUCK!

PUPPY LOVE

Use the clues and the grid to solve the puzzle. Draw an X in the boxes that can be eliminated and an O in the boxes that are a match. Remember: Every time you find an answer that is a match (O), cross out all choices vertically and horizontally in that category.

Five puppies are at the dog park. Use the clues to find out which type of dog each one is and to find out each puppy's favorite toy.

CLUES:

1. Neither Daisy, Rocky, nor Oliver are poodles, nor like the bear the best.

2. The beagle loves the chew toy the best, and the cocker spaniel loves the Frisbee.

3. The cocker spaniel doesn't like the tennis ball or the Frisbee the best.

4. Oliver and Sadie don't like toys that make noises, but the poodle loves them.

5. The border collie isn't named Daisy, Sadie, or Oliver, but loves the tennis ball the best.

6. Sadie is not a beagle, poodle, or cocker spaniel, but loves her stuffed animal toy.

	PUG	BEAGLE	POODLE	COCKER SPANIEL	BORDER COLLIE	FRISBEE	CHEW TOY	TENNIS BALL	SQUEAKY PIZZA	BEAR
DAISY										
ROCKY										
SADIE										
OLIVER										
LOLA										
FRISBEE										
CHEW TOY										
TENNIS BALL										
SQUEAKY PIZZA										
BEAR										

PUPPY FACT:

DALMATIAN PUPPIES ARE BORN WITH WHITE COATS BUT GET THEIR SPOTS IN ABOUT 3 TO 4 WEEKS!

ANSWERS ON PAGE 106

NAME: _____

Use the clues and the grid to solve the puzzle. Draw an X in the boxes that can be eliminated and an O in the boxes that are a match. Remember: Every time you find an answer that is a match (O), cross out all choices vertically and horizontally in that category.

Five friends take a trip to the Natural History Museum. Use the clues to find out which color backpack each one carried and each person's favorite exhibit.

CLUES:

1. Nico, Claire, and Brayton do not have a purple backpack.

2. Nala, who carries a red backpack, does not like insects or mummies.

3. The person with the gray backpack likes the mummy exhibit the best.

4. Brayton spent most of his time at the African shields exhibit. His backpack color starts with the same letter as his first name.

5. Neither Aiden nor Claire have a gray backpack.

6. Claire and Aiden spent the least amount of time at the mummy exhibit, but Claire bought a souvenir shark tooth.

	BLACK	GRAY	GREEN	PURPLE	RED	MUMMY	T-REX FOSSIL	INSECTS	SHARK TEETH	AFRICAN SHIELDS
NICO										
CLAIRE										
BRAYTON										
NALA										
AIDEN										
MUMMY										
T-REX FOSSIL										
INSECTS										
SHARK TEETH										
AFRICAN SHIELDS										

AT THE CARNIVAL

NAME: _____

Use the clues and the grid to solve the puzzle. Draw an X in the boxes that can be eliminated and an O in the boxes that are a match. Each time you find an answer that is a match (O), cross out all choices vertically and horizontally in that category.

Five brothers and sisters went to the carnival! Use the clues to find out which snack each one selected and which ride was each person's favorite.

CLUES:

1. Mateo didn't eat a snow cone or a corn dog. He rode the ride that starts with the same letter as his name.

2. Julia and Lucia like sweet treats, but Daniel and Mariana like salty ones.

3. The person who likes roller coasters ordered the cotton candy.

4. Mariana like rides that go around but doesn't like heights. Daniel likes a ride that goes up high to give him a view.

5. Lucia likes either roller coasters or swing rides. Julia likes either merry-go-round or swing rides.

6. Julia wanted a cold treat, while Daniel wanted something hot.

	CORN DOGS	COTTON CANDY	FUNNEL CAKE	SOFT PRETZEL	SNOW CONE	MERRY-GO-ROUND	FERRIS WHEEL	BUMPER CARS	SWING RIDE	ROLLER COASTER
MARIANA										
DANIEL										
LUCIA										
MATEO										
JULIA										
MERRY-GO-ROUND										
FERRIS WHEEL										
BUMPER CARS										
SWING RIDE										
ROLLER COASTER										

FERRIS WHEEL FACT:

THE FERRIS WHEEL WAS INVENTED BY GEORGE W. FERRIS FOR THE 1893 WORLD'S FAIR IN CHICAGO!

ANSWERS ON PAGE 106

TROPICAL FISH

NAME: —————————————————————

Use the clues and the grid to solve the puzzle. Draw an X in the boxes that can be eliminated and an O in the boxes that are a match. Each time you find an answer that is a match (O), cross out all choices vertically and horizontally in that category.

Five friends each have aquariums and want a new fish. Use the clues to find out which fish each one selected and what price each of them paid.

CLUES:

1. The angelfish, tiger barb, and goldfish didn't cost $2.00

2. Olivia spent $8.00 more than Ben.

3. None of the boys bought tiger barbs.

4. None of the girls bought zebra danios.

5. Hanna's fish was $4.00 less than Diego's fish.

6. Olivia didn't choose the tiger barb, the goldfish, or the angelfish.

7. Diego's fish was more expensive than Jake's fish.

	$2.00	$4.00	$6.00	$8.00	$10.00	ANGELFISH	TIGER BARB	KOI	GOLDFISH	ZEBRA DANIO
JAKE										
HANNA										
DIEGO										
OLIVIA										
BEN										
ANGELFISH										
TIGER BARB										
KOI										
GOLDFISH										
ZEBRA DANIO										

GOLDFISH FACT:

GOLDFISH LIVE THE LONGEST OF ANY AQUARIUM FISH. A GOLDFISH MAY LIVE UP TO 40 YEARS!

BRAIN BENDER

Use the clues and the grid to solve the puzzle.

Five friends decide to get their faces painted at an amusement park. Use the clues to find out which type of face painting, which color, and which price each of them paid.

CLUES:

1. The star costs $4.00 more than the emoji.
2. The hawk, shark, and car aren't red.
3. You could buy four of the green face paintings for the price of the gold.
4. Robert and Rose spent odd amounts of money but Rose spent more.
5. Erik and Robert both chose animals, and Courtney and Robert chose metallic colors.
6. Erik spent the least amount of money.
7. Neither Courtney nor Colleen chose the car.
8. Colleen's face painting cost $1.00 more than Robert's.
9. The blue one was more expensive than the red.
10. The shark was less expensive than the hawk.

	$2.00	$3.00	$4.00	$5.00	$8.00	RED	GOLD	SILVER	BLUE	GREEN	STAR	EMOJI	HAWK	SHARK	CAR
COURTNEY															
ERIK															
ROSE															
ROBERT															
COLLEEN															
STAR															
EMOJI															
HAWK															
SHARK															
CAR															
RED															
GOLD															
SILVER															
BLUE															
GREEN															

40

CHAPTER 5

CROSSWORDS TO CONSIDER

Crossword puzzles are a fun way to play with words you already know, while using letters and clues to learn some new ones too!

This chapter includes crosswords with a variety of themes, from coral reefs to fairy tales, the weather, and more! Just like all of the chapters, this chapter becomes more challenging as it moves along!

WHERE IN THE WORLD?

NAME: _____

Use the clues to complete this puzzle with all five oceans and seven continents.

ACROSS

3. Has the largest rainforest in the world (Amazon)
8. Has koalas, kangaroos, and crocodiles
9. Early European explorers crossed this ocean
10. The ocean between North/ South America and Asia
12. This ocean is the farthest north and is freezing cold

DOWN

1. A cold ocean near Antarctica
2. Continent with the bald eagle, the grizzly bear, and the Canada goose
4. A large continent with many countries like China and Russia
5. You might eat chocolate in Switzerland or pretzels in Germany on this continent
6. An ocean located between Africa and India
7. Has savannas with lions, elephants, and giraffes
11. No people live here except those in the space station

CONTINENT FACT:

ANTARCTICA IS THE ONLY CONTINENT WITHOUT ANY COUNTRIES!

ANSWERS ON PAGE 107

CORAL REEF

NAME: _____

Use the clues to complete this puzzle with coral reef sea creatures.

ACROSS

3. Snake-like fish that lives in small caves in the coral

4. Has a soft body between its two shells

5. Some live on land and some in the ocean, but all of them carry shells on their backs

9. Squishy creatures with 10 arms that swim quickly

10. Swims upright and has a long curly tail

11. Fish with sharp teeth but no bones, only cartilage

12. Usually have five arms and are also called sea stars

13. Has eight legs and eats clams and shrimp

DOWN

1. Has stinging tentacles

2. Poisonous fish, also called a pufferfish

6. Hard-shelled creatures with big front claws

7. Has eyes on stalks and a hard shell, and walks sideways

8. White and orange fish that lives with sea anemones

PUFFERFISH FACT:

A PUFFERFISH MAY LOOK CUTE, BUT ONE CONTAINS ENOUGH POISON TO KILL 30 ADULTS!

ANSWERS ON PAGE 107

IT'S ABOUT TIME

NAME: _____

Use the clues to complete this puzzle with time-related words.

ACROSS

4. People wear this small watch on their wrists

6. Seven of these in a week

9. Sixty of these in one minute

12. This is 12:00 in the daytime

13. A clock in a tall wooden cabinet that chimes

15. A German clock with tiny wooden birds that sing out on the hour

DOWN

1. Twelve of these in one year

2. How long the Earth takes to orbit the sun

3. No hands on this electronic clock

4. Starts on Sunday and ends on Saturday, seven days

5. Twenty-four of these in one day

7. One hundred years

8. Sixty of these in one hour

9. Was used to tell time before clocks were invented

10. This is 12:00 at night

11. Set this clock to help you wake up

14. Ten years

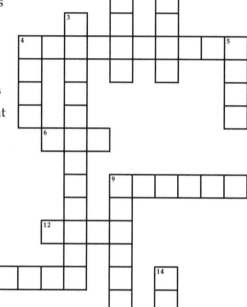

HOURGLASS FACT:

WHEN MAGELLAN SAILED AROUND THE WORLD IN 1519, HIS FLEET HAD 18 HOURGLASSES PER SHIP TO KEEP TIME!

ANSWERS ON PAGE 107

FRUITY FUN

NAME: _____

Use the clues to complete this puzzle with names of fruits.

DOWN

1. Red fruit with hundreds of tiny seeds on the outside
2. Large fruit that's green on the outside and red on the inside
3. Looks and tastes similar to a peach but its skin is smooth
6. Hawaiian fruit that's yellow on the inside
7. Orange fruit that makes a favorite breakfast juice
9. Long fruit that's white on the inside and has a yellow peel when it's ready to eat
13. Can be red, yellow, or green on the outside and is white on the inside

ACROSS

4. Fuzzy fruit that's orange on the inside and has a pit
5. Tart fruit that's yellow and is the size of a softball
8. Fuzzy brown on the outside and green on the inside
10. Tan and rough on the outside and orange on the inside
11. Purple fruit that was Little Jack Horner's favorite
12. Grows on vines, comes in bunches, and may be green or purple
14. Yellow fruit that's tart but is often made into a sweet drink

CRANBERRY FACT:

CRANBERRIES THAT ARE RIPE CAN BOUNCE! BOUNCING CRANBERRIES ARE SORTED BY MACHINES TO BE SOLD IN BAGS. THE REST ARE MADE INTO JUICE!

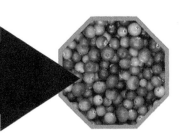

DESERT ANIMALS

NAME: _____

Use the clues to complete this puzzle with desert animals.

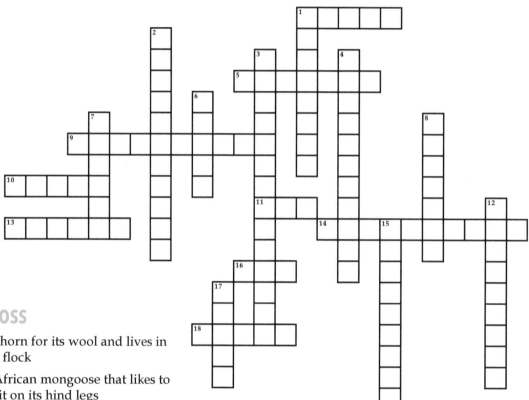

ACROSS

1. Shorn for its wool and lives in a flock
5. African mongoose that likes to sit on its hind legs
9. Fast-moving bird that prefers running to flying
10. Tropical lizard with pads on its feet
11. Nocturnal bird of prey with large eyes
13. Stubborn animal related to the horse
14. Blood-sucking, flying mammal that is nocturnal
16. Sly animal with a bushy tail
18. Has hooves and a hump on its back

DOWN

1. Poisonous with a stinger in its tail
2. Small hopping rodent
3. Large burrowing tortoise
4. Poisonous reptile that makes a rattling noise
6. Wild dog from Australia
7. Small dog-like animal related to the wolf
8. Large, bald scavenger bird
12. Large hairy spider
15. Large rodent with quills on its back
17. Woolly animal from South America

ROADRUNNER FACT:

ROADRUNNERS HAVE TWO TOES FACING FORWARD AND TWO TOES FACING BACKWARD ON EACH FOOT! THEY LEAVE "X"-SHAPED FOOTPRINTS!

ANSWERS ON PAGE 108

WHAT'S THE WEATHER?

NAME: _____

Use the clues to complete this puzzle with weather-related words.

ACROSS

2. Measures the temperature
3. Rumbling noise heard after lightning, due to expanding air
6. Flash of light in the sky, due to electrical charges
10. Low-lying cloud makes it hard to see long distances
11. Rain, snow, sleet, or hail that falls to the ground
12. This happens when a gas is turned into a liquid
13. Severe snowstorm with strong winds
14. Sits on roofs and shows wind direction
15. Measures rain

DOWN

1. When water vapor gathers together in the sky, this forms
2. Destructive funnel-shaped wind
4. Arch of colors in the sky after it rains
5. The study of weather
7. Violent spinning storm from warm oceans
8. When the sun warms water droplets and they change to a gas and rise
9. Moving air

TORNADO FACT:

TORNADOES MAY HAPPEN DURING ANY TIME OF THE DAY BUT THE MOST COMMON TIME IS 4:00 TO 9:00 PM!

ONCE UPON A TIME

NAME: _____

Use the clues to complete this puzzle with fairy tale titles.

ACROSS

1. A poor woman wants a child and a fairy gives her a seed that becomes a tiny baby, the size of a thumb.

2. She pricks her finger on a spinning wheel and is fast asleep until a prince kisses her.

7. When a brother is frozen by an evil wintry witch, his sister melts the ice in his heart with her tears.

10. A brother and sister find a candy house in the woods that belongs to an evil witch.

11. A mermaid longs to become a human and to leave the sea.

12. He plants magical seeds and climbs to the Giant's home in the sky.

13. With a fairy godmother's help, a hard-working young woman attends a ball.

DOWN

1. A young woman must prove she is a real princess by sleeping on a stack of mattresses with a hidden pea.

3. A poor man with a good heart wakes to find brand new shoes made by tiny workers.

4. A bird raised with ducks believes it is unattractive until it becomes a swan.

5. A girl is locked in a tower and escapes with the help of her long hair and a prince.

6. The wicked queen is after her but she hides in a cottage with seven miners.

8. When the miller's daughter is told to spin gold, a little man with a mysterious name helps.

9. An arrogant prince is turned into a beast and a young woman helps him change.

ANSWERS ON PAGE 108

GEOLOGY

Use the clues to complete this puzzle with geology-related words.

ACROSS

3. When land is worn down by water, wind, and ice
5. Large amount of dirt or mud sliding down a mountain
7. A vent in the Earth's crust that spews lava
9. Remains of an animal or plant from long ago
11. The process by which rocks are made and changed
12. Layer of earth between the crust and the core
13. Flat-topped hill
15. Large flat area with few trees
17. When plates collide at fault lines, it causes shaking
18. Narrow valley surrounded by steep cliffs

DOWN

1. Outer layer of the Earth
2. Center of the Earth
4. Loose layer over Earth's crust, often called dirt
5. Natural feature of the Earth's surface
6. Large chunks of the Earth's crust that sometimes collide
7. Low area between hills or mountains
8. Solid, natural material made from minerals
10. Solid layer of rock under the loose soil
12. Bigger than a hill, a large raised area
14. Small pieces of rocks, shells, and soil
16. Molten rock from a volcano

BRAIN BENDER

NAME: _____

This puzzle is filled with words that have silent letters and tricky spellings! Use the clues (and the word bank if you'd like) to solve the puzzle.

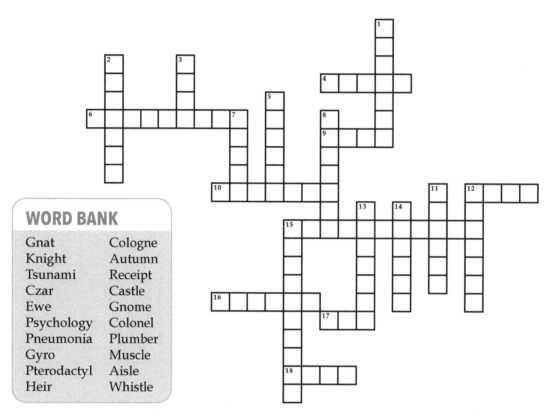

WORD BANK

Gnat
Knight
Tsunami
Czar
Ewe
Psychology
Pneumonia
Gyro
Pterodactyl
Heir

Cologne
Autumn
Receipt
Castle
Gnome
Colonel
Plumber
Muscle
Aisle
Whistle

ACROSS

4. Small mythical person who guards treasure underground

6. Illness involving the lungs

9. A person who inherits something after a family member dies

10. Paper showing items purchased

12. Russian emperor before 1917

15. Winged dinosaur from the Jurassic period

16. Soldier who served lords and kings in the Middle Ages

17. Female sheep

18. Small fly

DOWN

1. Person who fixes sinks and toilets

2. Tidal wave often caused by an earthquake

3. Greek sandwich

5. Tissue that helps the body move

7. Row in the grocery store

8. High-pitched sound made using the teeth and lips

11. The season when leaves fall

12. Military officer with a high rank

13. Similar to perfume

14. Home and fortress of a king and queen

15. The study of the human mind

ANSWERS ON PAGE 108

CHAPTER 6

WHIMSICAL WORDS

Rebus puzzles often use words in a clever way to represent common phrases or sayings. To solve rebus puzzles, you'll need to look at the position of the words carefully to decipher the meaning!

In this chapter you'll find lots of different rebus puzzles with themes like food, animals, school, and more. Some of the puzzles will seem easier, while others will be more challenging!

NAME: _____

Each puzzle shows a word picture of a common word or phrase.
Solve each puzzle and write the answer underneath.

1.

BLANKPIGET

_____

2.

COOKIES
+
MILK

_____

3.

G ^{S} G E

_____

4.

MARMALADE

_____

5.

BANANA

_____

6.

3.14159

_____

IT'S A ZOO IN HERE!

NAME: _____

Each puzzle shows a word picture of a common word or phrase.
Solve each puzzle and write the answer underneath.

1.

BIGfishPOND

_____

2.

_____

3.

DOG
DOG
DOG

_____

4.

LIFE   LIFE   LIFE
LIFE   LIFE   LIFE
LIFE   LIFE   LIFE

_____

5.

_____

6.

HERRING

_____

NAME: _____

Each puzzle shows a word picture of a common word or phrase.
Solve each puzzle and write the answer underneath.

1.

MOONCE**ON**

_____

2.

~~SAND~~

_____

3.

AIR
↑

_____

4.

_____

5.

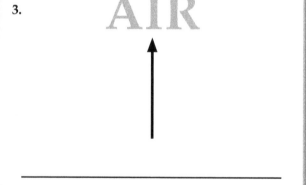

_____

6.

NATURE
NATURE◄
NATURE

_____

54

NAME: _____

Each puzzle shows a word picture of a common word or phrase.
Solve each puzzle and write the answer underneath.

1.

WHEEL

_____

2.

R O A D S
    D
  A
R O A D S
R   D S

_____

3.

B
R
O
K
E
N

_____

4.

◄STREET
STREET►

_____

5.

CART HORSE

_____

6.

WHEELER
WHEELER
WHEELER
WHEELER

_____

NAME: _____

Each puzzle shows a word picture of a common word or phrase.
Solve each puzzle and write the answer underneath.

1.

HAI
RS

_____

2.

CHETONGUEEK

_____

3.

THUMBS

↑

_____

4.

HEAD
HEEL HEEL

_____

5.

YOUR NOSE
―――――――――
RIGHT

_____

6.

5
SENSE SENSE

_____

ANSWERS ON PAGE 109

NAME: _____

Each puzzle shows a word picture of a common word or phrase.
Solve each puzzle and write the answer underneath.

1.
LEARN

_____

2. RED   GREEN
BLUE

PASS

_____

3.
1   2   3   4

_____

4.
READING BOOKS

_____

5.
$$\frac{ONE}{1\ HELP}$$

_____

6.
BRAIN   +   BRAIN

_____

NAME: _____

Each puzzle shows a word picture of a common word or phrase.
Solve each puzzle and write the answer underneath.

1.

**BITTEN
SHY
SHY**

_____

2.

_____

3.

P O D
PP

_____

4.

**ONE ONE ONE
ONE ONE ONE
DOZEN**

_____

5.

**STRAW
STRAW
STRAW
STRAW** ←

_____

6.

LIFE | DEATH

_____

ANSWERS ON PAGE 109

NAME: _____

Each puzzle shows a word picture of a common word or phrase.
Solve each puzzle and write the answer underneath.

1.

DAYSALLWORK

_____

2.

HEAD

WATER

_____

3.

POWER   POWER

_____

4.

_____

5.

THINK

_____

6.

DECISION

DECISION

_____

BRAIN BENDER

NAME: _____

Each puzzle shows a word picture of a common word or phrase.
Solve each puzzle and write the answer underneath.

1.
CUT CUT
_____
CUT CUT

2.

WIRE
_____

3.
AREA
_____

4.
CHINA SHOP BULL
_____

5.
LI CK E TY
_____

6.

TURN
_____

7.
FEET
FEET
_____

8.
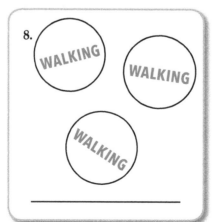
WALKING WALKING WALKING
_____

9.
COLLAR
HOT
_____

ANSWERS ON PAGE 109

CHAPTER 7

MINDFUL MATH

Sudoku and Mathdoku puzzles can be challenging but fun! To solve these puzzles, you'll need to notice patterns, keep careful track of number possibilities, and use persistence.

This chapter alternates Sudoku with Mathdoku. As you progress through the chapter, the puzzles will become a bit more complex!

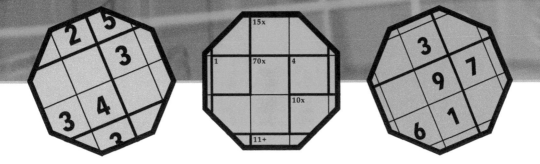

SUDOKU: LLAMA

NAME: _____

Fill in each empty cell (small box) with the numbers 1 to 4. Each number may only be used once in each row, once in each column, and once in each box (each group of four cells outlined in bolded print).

4		3	1
3			
			2
2	4		

1			3
3		2	
	3		2
2			4

2			3
	3	1	
	2	3	
3			1

		2	
	2		4
2		1	
	1		

LLAMA FACT:

LLAMA FARMERS CALL LLAMA MANURE "LLAMA BEANS." LLAMAS MAKE A FERTILIZER THAT IS ALMOST ODORLESS!

ANSWERS ON PAGE 109

MATHDOKU: YO-YO

Mathdoku is very similar to Sudoku! Fill in each empty cell (small box) with the numbers 1 to 4. Each number may only be used once in each row and once in each column.

The bolded areas are called cages. Each cage has a target number (the answer of the math problem) and an operation (addition, subtraction, multiplication, or division). If there is no operation sign by the target number, simply write the number shown in the cell.

Puzzle 1

24x		4	3+
	4+		
8+	2	3-	
		5+	

Puzzle 2

9+		2-	
12x		7+	1
			8x
	4÷		

Puzzle 3

24x			1
1	2-		5+
8+			
4+		6+	

Puzzle 4

1-	6+		3
		2-	7+
11+		4+	
			2

NAME: _____

Fill in each empty cell (small box) with the numbers 1 to 6. Each number may only be used once in each row, once in each column, and once in each box (each group of six cells outlined in bolded print).

6					2
		2	5	6	
2			3		5
	3	4			
1		3			4
	5		1		

For the Baby: Fill in each empty cell with the numbers 1 to 4. Each number may only be used once in each row, once in each column, and once in each box (each group of 4 cells outlined in bolded print).

3		1	4
4			
			3
2	3		

PANDA FACT:

ANSWERS ON PAGE 110

MATHDOKU: SPINNING TOPS

NAME: _____

Fill in each empty cell (small box) with the numbers 1 to 6. Each number may only be used once in each row and once in each column.

Each cage (bolded area) has a target number (the answer of the math problem) and the operation (+, -, x, or ÷). If there is no operation sign by the target number, simply write the number shown in the cell.

40x			1	2÷	
6+	6	15x		12x	60x
	20x	1	6		
		8+	5+		
11+	3÷			10x	4÷
		18x			

For the smaller Mathdoku: Fill in each empty cell with the numbers 1 to 4. Each number may only be used once in each row and once in each column.

32x		3÷	
	1	1-	
9x	2÷		4÷
		2	

SUDOKU: GIRAFFE

NAME: _____

Fill in each empty cell (small box) with the numbers 1 to 8. Each number may only be used once in each row, once in each column, and once in each box (each group of eight cells outlined in bolded print).

1					7	6	
		7	5	1			2
2			3		1		8
	1	8				4	
4		5			3		
3	2		8			7	
	5		6		2		4
8		2		6			7

GIRAFFE FACT:

GIRAFFES MAY HAVE LONG NECKS, BUT THEY HAVE THE SAME NUMBER OF VERTEBRAE (NECK BONES) THAT PEOPLE DO!

ANSWERS ON PAGE 110

MATHDOKU: BOOMERANG

NAME: _____

Fill in each empty cell (small box) with the numbers 1 to 8. Each number may only be used once in each row and once in each column.

Each cage (bolded area) has a target number (the answer of the math problem) and the operation (+, -, x, or ÷). If there is no operation sign by the target number, simply write the number shown in the cell.

2÷		5+		30x	7	5÷	
5-	18x	1	56x		4	5-	
				48x	15+		
15+	2	15x			7÷		4
	1	70x	4		60x		56x
			10+			3	
8+	4	11+		8+	8	3+	
	28x		8		18x		2

SUDOKU: KANGAROO

NAME: _____

Fill in each empty cell (small box) with the numbers 1 to 9. Each number may only be used once in each row, once in each column, and once in each box (each group of nine cells outlined in bolded print).

	3	9		8		2		
8			6		7		3	5
		5				1		
	9		2				7	4
5		4		7		8		
	6		4		3			2
		1			9	7		
3				6	1			8
9	8	6		4			5	1

KANGAROO FACT:

KANGAROOS HOP EVERYWHERE, BUT THEY CAN'T HOP BACKWARD! THEIR LONG TAIL MAKES IT IMPOSSIBLE!

ANSWERS ON PAGE 110

MATHDOKU: ROBOT

NAME: _____

Fill in each empty cell (small box) with the numbers 1 to 9. Each number may only be used once in each row and once in each column.

Each cage (bolded area) has a target number (the answer of the math problem) and the operation (+, -, x, or ÷). If there is no operation sign by the target number, simply write the number shown in the cell.

54x			120x	7	80x		13+	7÷
2÷		6÷		5		9		
7	13+			16x	9÷	1		8
72x						270x		
	2	40x	1	3÷	17+		70x	
4+	6		96x		11+			3
				8		10x	15+	
6	100x	63x		4+			4-	
		9	13+		8	6+		

BRAIN BENDER

NAME: _____

Fill in each empty cell (small box) with the numbers 1 to 9. Each number may only be used once in each row, once in each column, and once in each box (each group of nine cells outlined in bolded print).

3				2		1		
	4	8			5			7
	1		6					3
	5	6	2		3	7		
				1		2	6	
9	2	7	4					5
8			7	6				1
		1			9	8		
	9	2		5		6	3	

ANSWERS ON PAGE 110

CHAPTER 8

CURI_US CRYPT_GRAMS

Cryptograms take a bit of detective work! You'll be given a few letter clues, but will then be asked to solve the rest of the puzzle using your own knowledge of words and phrases and a bit of logic.

This chapter includes cryptograms with fun themes like castles, pizza, and Mount Everest! Don't forget, the puzzles will become more challenging as you move along.

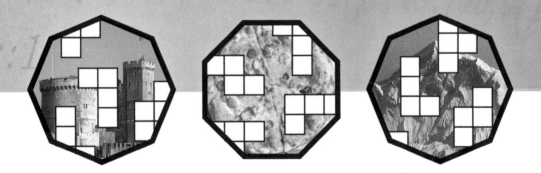

BASKETBALL FACTS

NAME: _____

Solve the cryptogram by finding a number for each letter. Not all letters will be used in each puzzle.

A	B	C	D	E	F	G	H	I	J	K	L	M	N	O	P	Q	R	S	T	U	V	W	X	Y	Z
7				8									17				18								

$\overline{1}\ \overline{7}\ \overline{12}\ \overline{3}\ \overline{8}\ \overline{24}\ \overline{1}\ \overline{7}\ \overline{10}\ \overline{10}$ $\quad$ $\overline{25}\ \overline{7}\ \overline{12}$ $\quad$ $\overline{21}\ \overline{17}\ \overline{19}\ \overline{8}\ \overline{17}\ \overline{24}\ \overline{8}\ \overline{20}$

$\overline{20}\ \overset{R}{\overline{5}}\ \overset{}{\overline{18}}\ \overline{21}\ \overset{N}{\overline{17}}\ \overline{15}$ $\quad$ $\overline{25}\ \overline{21}\ \overset{N}{\overline{17}}\ \overline{24}\ \overset{E}{\overline{8}}\ \overset{R}{\overline{18}}$ $\quad$ $\overset{A}{\overline{7}}\ \overline{12}$ $\quad$ $\overset{A}{\overline{7}}\ \overset{N}{\overline{17}}$

$\overline{21}\ \overset{N}{\overline{17}}\ \overline{20}\ \overline{11}\ \overline{11}\ \overset{R}{\overline{18}}$ $\quad$ $\overline{15}\ \overset{A}{\overline{7}}\ \overline{22}\ \overset{E}{\overline{8}}$.

A	B	C	D	E	F	G	H	I	J	K	L	M	N	O	P	Q	R	S	T	U	V	W	X	Y	Z
	8			12		23									2		19			26					

$\overset{P}{\overline{2}}\ \overline{4}\ \overline{5}\ \overline{6}\ \overset{H}{\overline{23}}$ $\quad$ $\overset{B}{\overline{8}}\ \overset{S}{\overline{5}}\ \overline{19}\ \overline{14}\ \overline{4}\ \overline{9}\ \overset{S}{\overline{19}}$ $\quad$ $\overset{W}{\overline{26}}\ \overline{4}\ \overline{1}\ \overline{4}$ $\quad$ $\overline{24}\ \overset{S}{\overline{19}}\ \overline{4}\ \overline{16}$

$\overline{5}\ \overset{S}{\overline{19}}$ $\quad$ $\overline{9}\ \overset{H}{\overline{23}}\ \overline{4}$ $\quad$ $\overset{F}{\overline{12}}\ \overline{3}\ \overline{1}\ \overset{S}{\overline{19}}\ \overline{9}$ $\quad$ $\overset{B}{\overline{8}}\ \overline{5}\ \overset{S}{\overline{19}}\ \overline{14}\ \overline{4}\ \overline{9}\ \overline{8}\ \overline{5}\ \overline{21}\ \overline{21}$

$\overset{H}{\overline{23}}\ \overline{25}\ \overline{25}\ \overset{P}{\overline{2}}\ \overset{S}{\overline{19}}$.

ANSWERS ON PAGE 110

NAME: —————————————

Solve the cryptogram by finding a number for each letter. Not all letters will be used in each puzzle.

A	B	C	D	E	F	G	H	I	J	K	L	M	N	O	P	Q	R	S	T	U	V	W	X	Y	Z
			2	9							18						21		5						

D _ ' **T**   _ _ _ _ **T**   _ _ _ **R**
2 25 4 5   24 25 20 4 5   6 25 20 21

_ _ _ _ **E** _ _ _   _ _ **T** _ **L**
24 1 8 24 3 9 4 14   20 4 5 8 18

T _ **E** _ ' **R E**   _ _ **T** _ _ **E D** .
5 1 9 6 21 9   1 10 5 24 1 9 2

A	B	C	D	E	F	G	H	I	J	K	L	M	N	O	P	Q	R	S	T	U	V	W	X	Y	Z
							9	18									2							16	

_ **H** _ _ _ _ _ **R**   **Y** _ _   _ _ '
1 9 7 14 25 22 25 2   16 26 23   17 26

_ _   _ **I H**   _ _ _   **Y** _ _ **R**
17 26   1 18 14 9   7 20 20   16 26 23 2

_ **I** _ **H** _ .
3 18 21 2 14

CASTLES

NAME: _____

Solve the cryptogram by finding a number for each letter. Not all letters will be used in each puzzle.

A	B	C	D	E	F	G	H	I	J	K	L	M	N	O	P	Q	R	S	T	U	V	W	X	Y	Z
	15										21		12				4		11						

$\overline{11}\ \overline{2}\ \overline{7}$ $\overline{23}\ \overline{22}\ \overline{4}\ \overline{5}\ \overline{11}$ $\overline{1}\ \overline{6}\ \overline{5}\ \overline{11}\ \overline{21}\ \overline{7}\ \overline{5}$ $\overline{16}\ \overline{7}\ \overline{4}\ \overline{7}$

$\overset{B}{\overline{15}}\ \overline{10}\ \overset{L}{\overline{22}}\ \overset{}{\overline{21}}\ \overset{T}{\overline{11}}$ $\overset{O}{\overline{12}}\ \overline{23}$ $\overline{16}\ \overset{O}{\overline{12}}\ \overset{O}{\overline{12}}\ \overline{24}$, $\overset{B}{\overline{15}}\ \overline{10}\ \overset{T}{\overline{11}}$ $\overset{L}{\overline{21}}\ \overline{6}\ \overset{T}{\overline{11}}\ \overline{7}\ \overline{4}$

$\overset{T}{\overline{11}}\ \overline{2}\ \overline{7}\ \overline{19}$ $\overline{10}\ \overline{5}\ \overline{7}\ \overline{24}$ $\overline{5}\ \overset{T}{\overline{11}}\ \overset{O}{\overline{12}}\ \overline{9}\ \overline{7}$.

A	B	C	D	E	F	G	H	I	J	K	L	M	N	O	P	Q	R	S	T	U	V	W	X	Y	Z
		12		5							8		1					7							

$\overset{C}{\overline{12}}\ \overline{2}\ \overline{3}\ \overset{T}{\overline{7}}\ \overset{L}{\overline{8}}\ \overline{5}\ \overline{3}$ $\overline{23}\ \overset{E}{\overline{5}}\ \overline{21}\ \overset{E}{\overline{5}}$ $\overset{O}{\overline{1}}\ \overline{4}\ \overline{7}\ \overset{T}{\overline{5}}\ \overset{E}{\overline{20}}$ $\overline{6}\ \overline{22}\ \overline{10}\ \overset{L}{\overline{8}}\ \overset{T}{\overline{7}}$

$\overline{1}\ \overline{20}$ $\overset{T}{\overline{7}}\ \overset{E}{\overline{17}}\ \overline{5}$ $\overset{T}{\overline{7}}\ \overset{O}{\overline{1}}\ \overline{25}$ $\overset{O}{\overline{1}}\ \overline{4}$ $\overline{2}$ $\overline{17}\ \overline{10}\ \overset{L}{\overline{8}}\ \overset{L}{\overline{8}}$.

CASTLE FACT:

CASTLES HAD WALLS THAT WERE 3 TO 20 FEET THICK TO PROVIDE EXTRA PROTECTION AGAINST ENEMY ATTACKS!

ANSWERS ON PAGE 111

NAME: _____

Solve the cryptogram by finding a number for each letter. Not all letters will be used in each puzzle.

A	B	C	D	E	F	G	H	I	J	K	L	M	N	O	P	Q	R	S	T	U	V	W	X	Y	Z
4							14					9		15				22							

$$\underset{4}{\text{A}} \quad \underset{5}{\_}\,\underset{7}{\_}\,\underset{8}{\_}\,\underset{15}{\text{P}}\,\underset{14}{\text{H}}\,\underset{6}{\_}\,\underset{9}{\text{N}} \quad \underset{2}{\_}\,\underset{4}{\text{A}}\,\underset{22}{\text{T}}\,\underset{1}{\_} \quad \underset{4}{\text{A}}\,\underset{12}{\_}\,\underset{7}{\_}\,\underset{25}{\_}\,\underset{22}{\text{T}}$$

$$\underset{22}{\text{T}}\,\underset{14}{\text{H}}\,\underset{6}{\_}\,\underset{21}{\_}\,\underset{22}{\text{T}}\,\underset{18}{\_} \quad \underset{15}{\text{P}}\,\underset{7}{\_}\,\underset{25}{\_}\,\underset{9}{\text{N}}\,\underset{5}{\_}\,\underset{1}{\_} \quad \underset{7}{\_}\,\underset{26}{\_} \quad \underset{26}{\_}\,\underset{6}{\_}\,\underset{1}{\_}\,\underset{14}{\text{H}}$$

$$\underset{2}{\_}\,\underset{4}{\text{A}}\,\underset{3}{\_}\,\underset{14}{\text{H}} \quad \underset{5}{\_}\,\underset{4}{\text{A}}\,\underset{18}{\_} \; .$$

A	B	C	D	E	F	G	H	I	J	K	L	M	N	O	P	Q	R	S	T	U	V	W	X	Y	Z
		10						8					4				5			20				13	

$$\underset{3}{\_}\,\underset{4}{\text{O}}\,\underset{11}{\_}\,\underset{22}{\_}\,\underset{2}{\_}\,\underset{8}{\text{I}}\,\underset{21}{\_}\,\underset{5}{\text{S}} \quad \underset{9}{\_}\,\underset{15}{\_}\,\underset{1}{\_} \quad \underset{5}{\text{S}}\,\underset{4}{\text{O}}\,\underset{10}{\text{C}}\,\underset{8}{\text{I}}\,\underset{9}{\_}\,\underset{11}{\_}$$

$$\underset{9}{\_}\,\underset{21}{\_}\,\underset{8}{\text{I}}\,\underset{16}{\_}\,\underset{9}{\_}\,\underset{11}{\_}\,\underset{5}{\text{S}} \; , \quad \underset{5}{\text{S}}\,\underset{4}{\text{O}} \quad \underset{14}{\_}\,\underset{2}{\_}\,\underset{1}{\_}\,\underset{13}{\text{Y}} \quad \underset{11}{\_}\,\underset{8}{\text{I}}\,\underset{20}{\text{V}}\,\underset{1}{\_} \quad \underset{9}{\_}\,\underset{21}{\_}\,\underset{3}{\_}$$

$$\underset{2}{\_}\,\underset{6}{\_}\,\underset{21}{\_}\,\underset{14}{\_} \quad \underset{8}{\text{I}}\,\underset{21}{\_} \quad \underset{17}{\_}\,\underset{15}{\_}\,\underset{4}{\text{O}}\,\underset{6}{\_}\,\underset{22}{\_}\,\underset{5}{\text{S}} \; .$$

DOLPHIN FACT:

A DOLPHIN SLEEPS ON THE SURFACE OF THE WATER, SO IT CAN BREATHE. IT SLEEPS WITH ONE EYE OPEN AND HALF OF ITS BRAIN WIDE AWAKE!

NAME: _____

Solve the cryptogram by finding a number for each letter. Not all letters will be used in each puzzle.

A	B	C	D	E	F	G	H	I	J	K	L	M	N	O	P	Q	R	S	T	U	V	W	X	Y	Z
				19			8					13	26						17						

M _ _ **E** _ _ **H** _ **N** _ _ **E** _ **E N** _ **M** _ _ _ _ _ **N**
13 3 12 19   11 8 7 26   4 19 25 19 26   13 9 2 2 9 3 26

_ **E** _ _ **E** _ **E** _ _ _ _ _ _ **H** _ _ _ **M U** _
23 19 3 23 2 19   25 9 4 9 11   11 8 9 4   1 7 13 3 17 4

M _ **N U M E N** _ _ **E** _ **H** _ _ **E** _ _ .
13 3 26 17 13 19 26 11   19 7 20 8   16 19 7 12

A	B	C	D	E	F	G	H	I	J	K	L	M	N	O	P	Q	R	S	T	U	V	W	X	Y	Z
							18	10						2					26		12				

I T _ **T O O** _ _ **T H** _ _ _ _ **H** _ _ _ _ _ _ _
10 26   26 2 2 7   26 18 25 17 17   18 23 21 9 25 17 9

W O _ _ _ _ _ _ _ **O** _ **T** _ **T W O** _ _ _ _ _
12 2 25 7 17 25 1   3 4 2 23 26   26 12 2   13 17 3 25 1

T O _ _ **I** _ _ _ **T H** _ _ **I** _ _ _ _ _ **T O W** _ _ .
26 2   4 23 10 20 9   26 18 17   17 10 5 5 17 20   26 2 12 17 25

ANSWERS ON PAGE 111

NAME: _____

Solve the cryptogram by finding a number for each letter. Not all letters will be used in each puzzle.

A	B	C	D	E	F	G	H	I	J	K	L	M	N	O	P	Q	R	S	T	U	V	W	X	Y	Z
7				11														25		12					

E __ __ __ __ __ __ __ S __ A __ S E __ __ A S __
11 21 19 2 3 10 24 22 25   14 7 22   25 11 22 5   7 25 6

__ V E __ S E V E __ E E __ __ __ __ E S __ __
24 12 11 21   25 11 12 11 22 3 11 11 22   9 10 1 11 25   10 22

__ __ E __ A __ __ .
3 6 11   7 10 21

A	B	C	D	E	F	G	H	I	J	K	L	M	N	O	P	Q	R	S	T	U	V	W	X	Y	Z
				4	25			9							24		2								

__ __ __ __ __ F __ __ E __ __ R __ ' __ I __ __ __ E __
14 1 13 21   1 25   21 3 4   6 1 2 10 22 13   16 9 15 15 4 13 21

E R __ P __ I __ __ __ __ P P E __ I __
4 2 7 24 21 9 1 18 13   3 8 24 24 4 18   9 18

__ __ E __ P __ __ I F I __ __ R I __ __ __ F __ F I R E .
21 3 4   24 8 5 9 25 9 5   2 9 18 15   1 25   25 9 2 4

SAND FACT:

SOME ISLANDS, LIKE HAWAII AND ICELAND, HAVE BLACK SAND BEACHES! THE SAND IS MADE FROM PIECES OF LAVA THAT HAVE BROKEN DOWN.

PIZZA

NAME: _____

Solve the cryptogram by finding a number for each letter. Not all letters will be used in each puzzle.

A	B	C	D	E	F	G	H	I	J	K	L	M	N	O	P	Q	R	S	T	U	V	W	X	Y	Z
	12		21											19			14				5	16			6

```
  O           R            V                   B                    O             Z Z
 19   5    1   14       20  10  5   1       12  10  2   2  10  19  18      3  10  6   6   7   4

      R               O                W   O   R        W                          
  7  14   1        4  19   2  21      16  19  14   2   21  16  10  21   1        1   7   8   9

          R  .
 23   1    7  14
```

A	B	C	D	E	F	G	H	I	J	K	L	M	N	O	P	Q	R	S	T	U	V	W	X	Y	Z
4			6								9				1			15							

```
              S                P       P       L   A            P               A
 11  13   5        18  22  15  11      1  22   1  17   9   4  10      1   8   3   3   4

  D       L                           D   A       S        A            A   L   L
  6   5   9   8  23   5  10  26        6   4  26  15        4  10   5    13   4   9   9  22  16   5   5   2

  A   D       S   P                          L        S           D   A  .
  4   2   6  15  17   1   5  10       12  22  16   9       15  17   2   6   4  26
```

ANSWERS ON PAGE 112

NAME: _____

Solve the cryptogram by finding a number for each letter. Not all letters will be used in each puzzle.

A	B	C	D	E	F	G	H	I	J	K	L	M	N	O	P	Q	R	S	T	U	V	W	X	Y	Z
		21		20							3		13			26			24						

    O R   T   O R   T   O
__ __ __ __   __ __ __ __   __ __ __ __   __ __ __ __ __ __ __ __
9 13 26 20   24 1 5 6   10 13 14 26   24 1 13 14 4 5 6 2

           E   C C E   L L   C L   E
__ __ __ __   __ __ __ __ __ __ __ __ __ __ __ __   __ __ __ __ __ __ __
1 5 7 20   4 14 21 21 20 4 4 10 14 3 3 8   21 3 12 9 11 20 2

  T O   T   E   T O   O   T   E   O   T
__ __   __ __ __   __ __ __   __ __   __ __ __   __ __ __ __ __ __ __ .
24 13   24 1 20   24 13 17   13 10   24 1 20   9 13 14 6 24 5 12 6

A	B	C	D	E	F	G	H	I	J	K	L	M	N	O	P	Q	R	S	T	U	V	W	X	Y	Z
			8					1			2	12	3						5						

      M   T   E   M M I T   N
__ __ __ __   __ __ __   __ __ __ __ __ __ ,   __ __ __   __ __ __
16 19 18 12   5 22 8   21 24 12 12 1 5 ,   14 18 24   7 6 3

  E E   T I   E T   I N   I   N
__ __ __   __ __ __ __ __ ,   __ __ __ __ __ ,   __ __ __
21 8 8   5 1 11 8 5 ,   1 3 17 1 6 ,   6 3 17

  N E   L
__ __ __ __ .
3 8 4 6 2

NAME: _____

All of the cryptograms listed are inventions. Some were earth-changing inventions, while others were smaller, yet still important! Solve each separate cryptogram by finding a number for each letter.

A	B	C	D	E	F	G	H	I	J	K	L	M	N	O	P	Q	R	S	T	U	V	W	X	Y	Z
		17	1		26						14							16			11				

W __ __ __ __ __ G
11 7 13 6 10 22 26

__ __ __ __ __ __ C E
2 7 17 6 10 22 1

C __ __
17 7 9

T E L E __ __ __ __ E
16 1 14 1 12 6 8 22 1

__ __ __ E __
12 7 12 1 9

W __ E E L
11 6 1 1 14

__ __ __ __ T __ G
12 9 10 22 16 10 22 26

__ __ E __ __
12 9 1 13 13

C __ __ __ __ __ __
17 8 2 12 7 13 13

L __ G T __ __ L __
14 10 26 6 16 5 3 14 5

C __ __ __ T E __
17 8 2 12 3 16 1 9

__ __ __ __ L __ E __
7 10 9 12 14 7 22 1

T E L E __ C __ __ E
16 1 14 1 13 17 8 12 1

__ I __ C __ __ I T I __ I __ G
7 10 9 17 8 22 15 10 16 10 8 22 10 22 26

__ __ __
12 1 22

MIND YOUR MATCHSTICKS

Matchstick puzzles train your mind to imagine a number of possibilities before finding one that works. You can use pencil and paper to solve these, but if you're stuck, real matchsticks or small pieces of paper might be helpful!

This chapter includes a variety of matchstick puzzles with shapes, numbers, and equations. Just like all of the chapters, they'll start simple but will become more complex as you move along.

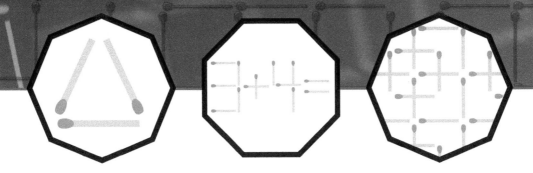

NAME: _____

1. Move 6 matchsticks to make the fish change direction.
   Draw your answer in the space provided.

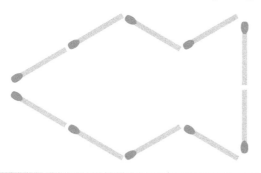

2. Move 3 matchsticks to make a large trapezoid.
   Draw your answer in the space provided.

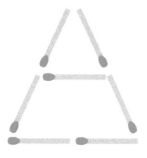

3. Move 3 matchsticks to make 4 triangles.
   Draw your answer in the space provided.

EAGLE EYES!

NAME: _____

1. Move 1 matchstick to make the equation true. Bonus if you can find two solutions! Draw your answer in the space provided.

0 + 5 = 1

2. Move 1 matchstick to make the equation true. Draw your answer in the space provided.

1 + 2 = 4

3. Move 1 matchstick to make the equation true. Draw your answer in the space provided.

3 + 4 = 5

NAME: _____

1. Move 3 matchsticks to make a stair structure ⌐▢ with squares and rectangles inside of it. Draw your answer in the space provided.

2. Add 4 matchsticks to make a total of 7 rectangles and 3 squares. Draw your answer in the space provided.

3. Move 4 matchsticks to make the chick into a fish with a square eye, a fin, and a tail. Draw your answer in the space provided.

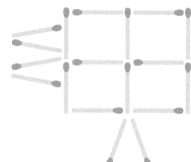

ANSWERS ON PAGE 113

NAME: _____

1. Move 2 matchsticks to make the inequality true.
   Draw your answer in the space provided.

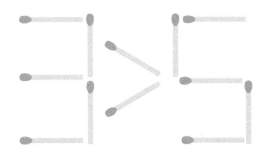

2. Move 1 matchstick to make the inequality true.
   Draw your answer in the space provided.

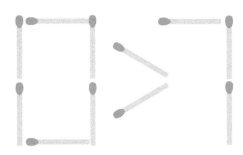

3. Move 1 matchstick to make the inequality true. Bonus points if you
   can think of two solutions! Draw your answer in the space provided.

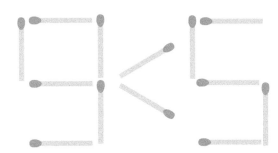

NAME: _____

---

1. Move 2 matchsticks to make 3 diamonds and 4 triangles.
   Draw your answer in the space provided.

---

2. Move 3 matchsticks to make 1 trapezoid and 1 diamond.
   Draw your answer in the space provided.

---

3. Move 6 matchsticks to make a "W" shape.
   Draw your answer in the space provided.

TRIANGLE FACT:

THE FLATIRON BUILDING, BUILT IN 1902 IN NEW
YORK CITY, IS A TRIANGULAR SKYSCRAPER! IT
WAS CALLED THE FLATIRON BECAUSE PEOPLE
THOUGHT IT LOOKED LIKE A CLOTHES IRON!

ANSWERS ON PAGE 114

NAME: _____

1. Move 3 matchsticks to make the equation true.
   Draw your answer in the space provided.

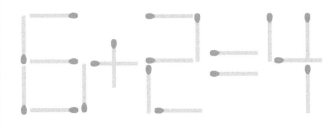

2. Move 2 matchsticks to make the equation true. Bonus if you can
   find two solutions. Draw your answer in the space provided.

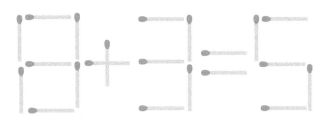

3. Move 2 matchsticks to make the equation true.
   Draw your answer in the space provided.

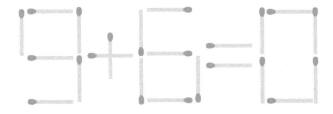

OWL FACT:

NAME: _____

1. Move 4 matchsticks to make 4 squares.
   Draw your answer in the space provided.

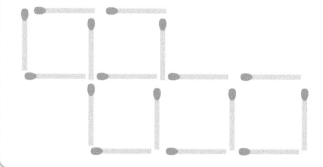

2. Move 4 matchsticks to make 5 squares.
   Draw your answer in the space provided.

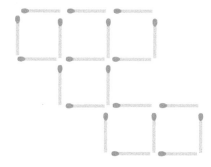

3. Move 8 matchsticks to make the cat into a sheep with an ear, a head (on the left side), and 4 legs. Draw your answer in the space provided.

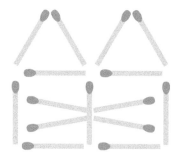

ANSWERS ON PAGE 114

NUMBER SCRAMBLE

1. Move 3 matchsticks to make the largest possible number. Draw your answer in the space provided.

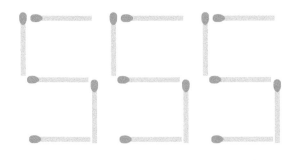

2. Move 3 matchsticks to make the smallest possible number, which doesn't start with zero. Draw your answer in the space provided.

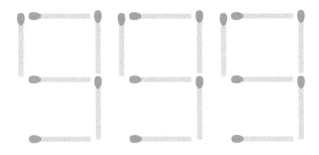

3. Move 3 matchsticks to make the largest possible number. Draw your answer in the space provided.

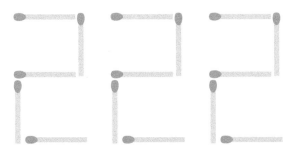

How many squares are there? _____

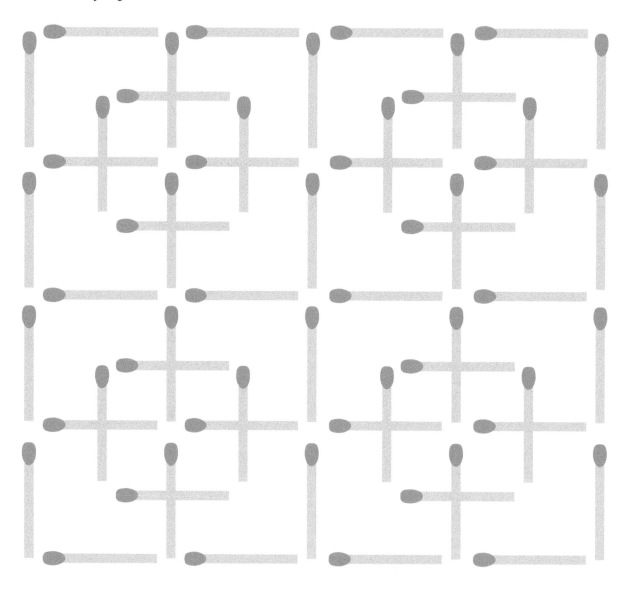

CHAPTER 10

ODD BIRDS

In these odd one out puzzles, almost all of the words, numbers, or pictures will go together in some way . . . except for one of them. Your job is to find the one that's different!

On the surface, it sounds easy, but some of these odd one out puzzles may be more challenging than you think, especially as the chapter progresses! Don't worry, though—by noticing similarities and differences and using a bit of logical reasoning, you'll be solving these puzzles in no time!

NAME: _____

Look at each object in the row. They all have something in common except one.
Circle the letter of the shape that doesn't belong.

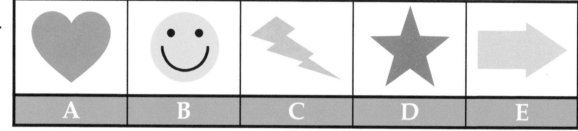

1.   A   B   C   D   E

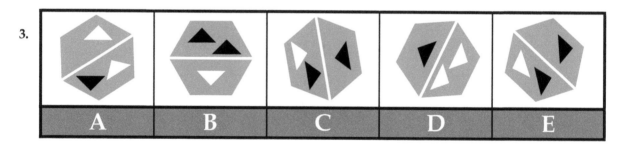

2.   A   B   C   D   E

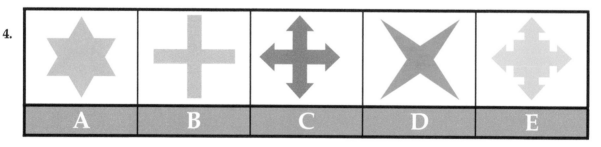

3.   A   B   C   D   E

4.   A   B   C   D   E

SHAPE FACT:

TRIANGLES ARE OFTEN USED IN CONSTRUCTION BECAUSE OF THEIR STRENGTH!

ANSWERS ON PAGE 115

A DOZEN DIFFERENCES

Look at the objects in each rectangle. They all have something in common except one. Circle the item that doesn't belong.

1.	2.	3.
ACD FHI RTU KMN VYZ	146 357 802 644 280	Planet Moon Crater Star Comet

4.	5.	6.
Dollar Quarter Penny Nickel Dime	1/4 .75 one fifth 1/2 two thirds	Gloomy Depressed Blue Thrilled Melancholy

7.	8.	9.
Frying pan Spatula Mixing bowl Rake Cookie sheet	Trumpet Guitar Violin Harp Cello	248 336 4416 5525 7749

10.	11.	12.
314 527 808 112 543	Eel Squid Octopus Whale Sand	Hip-hop Classical Clarinet Country Rock and roll

A DOZEN FACT:

EGGS ARE SOLD BY THE DOZEN BECAUSE IN FIRST-CENTURY ENGLAND, AN EGG WAS SOLD FOR A PENCE (LIKE A PENNY) OR 12 FOR A SHILLING (WHICH EQUALED 12 PENCE)!

SEEING SPOTS!

Look at each object in the row. They all have something in common except one.
Circle the letter of the shape that doesn't belong.

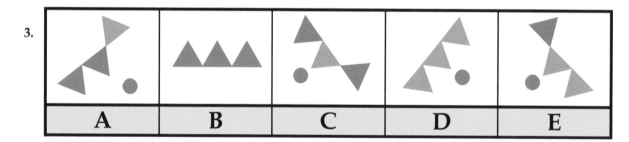

1.	A	B	C	D	E
2.	A	B	C	D	E
3.	A	B	C	D	E
4.	A	B	C	D	E

ANSWERS ON PAGE 115

WHICH ONE IS DIFFERENT?

NAME: _____

Look at the objects in each rectangle. They all have something in common except one. Circle the item that doesn't belong.

1.	2.	3.
Eagle Falcon Robin Owl Vulture	Addition Subtraction Multiplication Fractions Division	45 100 80 500 20

4.	5.	6.
Peninsula Crust Gulf Island Mountain	$\frac{5}{8}$ $\frac{4}{10}$ $\frac{3}{6}$ $\frac{1}{3}$ $\frac{5}{4}$	Meter Ounce Yard Inch Centimeter

7.	8.	9.
Soccer ball Pizza pan Globe Marbles Crystal ball	Paintbrush Markers Crayons Paints Sculpture	11 22 333 4444 55555

10.	11.	12.
A E B T W	Belt Hat Shirt Scarf Jewelry	Asia New Zealand Denmark Canada Argentina

DIFFERENT FACT:

SOMETIMES DIFFERENT ANIMALS ARE THE BEST OF FRIENDS, LIKE FRED THE LABRADOR AND DENNIS THE DUCKLING, BEA THE GIRAFFE AND WILMA THE OSTRICH, AND TORQUE THE DOG AND SHREK THE OWL!

FAIR AND SQUARE

Look at each object in the row. They all have something in common except one.
Circle the letter of the shape that doesn't belong.

1.

| A | B | C | D | E |

2.

| A | B | C | D | E |

3.

| A | B | C | D | E |

4.

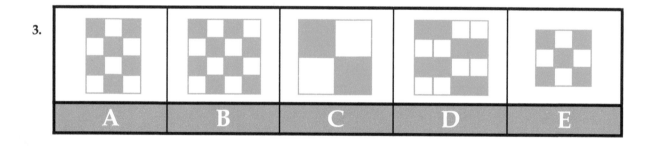

| A | B | C | D | E |

ANSWERS ON PAGE 115

NAME: _____

Look at the objects in each rectangle. They all have something in common except one.
Circle the item that doesn't belong.

1. Dalmatian Golden retriever Basset hound King Charles spaniel Red fox	**2.** Quarts Feet Pints Ounces Cups	**3.** 9 24 7 30 15
4. Picasso Monet Beethoven Michelangelo Van Gogh	**5.** $\frac{4}{8}$ $\frac{2}{4}$ $\frac{3}{7}$ $\frac{1}{2}$ $\frac{5}{10}$	**6.** Rain Hail Sleet Snow Freezing rain
7. Paris Miami Tokyo Mexico London	**8.** Triangle Piano Cymbals Tambourine Drums	**9.** .75 .42 3.5 .89 .51
10. N Y Z X K	**11.** Bowling Golf Billiards Tennis Badminton	**12.** Landslide Hurricane Volcano Tornado Mountain

FOOTBALL FACT:

FOOTBALL TEAMS USE UP TO
108 GAME BALLS AND 12 KICKER
BALLS AT THE SUPER BOWL!

ANSWERS ON PAGE 116

NAME: _____

Look at each object in the row. They all have something in common except one.
Circle the letter of the shape that doesn't belong.

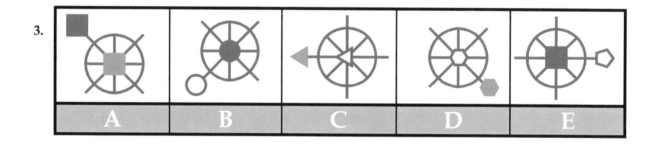

ANSWERS ON PAGE 116

SQUARE PEGS

NAME: _____

Look at the objects in each rectangle. They all have something in common except one. Circle the item that doesn't belong.

1. **Alligator** **Turtle** **Salamander** **Boa constrictor** **Iguana**	**2.** Cube Pyramid Cylinder Cone Trapezoid	**3.** **12 in. = 1 ft.** **16 oz. = 2 lb.** **1,000 gm. = 1 kg.** **2 pt. = 1 qt.** **100 cm. = 1 m.**
4. Limestone Granite Flint Quartz Steel	**5.** Democracy Buddhism Socialism Monarchy Communism	**6.** Grasshopper Spider Dragonfly Dung beetle Gnat
7. Fern Desert Tundra Rainforest Grasslands	**8.** **Bach** **Beethoven** **Mozart** **Handel** **Matisse**	**9.** 135 789 246 579 357
10. Hundreds Forty-fives Tens Thousands Ones	**11.** **Niagara Falls** **Tower of Pisa** **Grand Canyon** **Uluru Rock** **Mount Kilimanjaro**	**12.** Big Dipper Orion Leo Little Dipper Neutron star

ANSWERS ON PAGE 116

BRAIN BENDER

NAME: _____

Look at the objects and lists in each row. They all have something in common, except one. Circle the one in each row that doesn't belong.

1	2	3	4	5
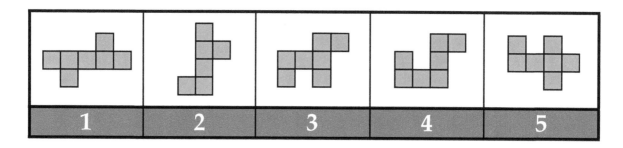

1	2	3	4	5
Euro Dollar Mint Peso Yen	Chemist Astronomer Paleontologist Accountant Zoologist	Blouse Beanie Beret Sombrero Fedora	Achieve Attempt Accomplish Fulfill Succeed	Engine Radiator Brakes Battery Screwdriver

1	2	3	4	5
$ N 8 V # M 4 A &	8 N $ & A 4 V # M	X H 6 % @ > 3 F O	8 N $ M # V & A 4	O F 3 > @ % 6 H X

1	2	3	4	5
4 25 64 11 100	At = 4 Apple = 10 Dog = 6 Mouse = 15 School = 12	25 dollars 25 pennies 1 quarter 5 nickels 1 dime 3 nickels	36 54 18 26 45	53142 25314 45317 34521 15342

ANSWERS ON PAGE 116

PATTERNS AT PLAY

2 Shape Mysteries

1.  **2.**  **3.**  **4.**  **5.**

3 Matrix Magic

1. 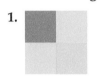 **2.** **3.**

4 Buzzing About Numbers

1. 45   50
2. 4   4
3. 50   5
4. 99   110
5. 256   512
6. 39   48

5 Copycat Patterns

1.

3.

2.

4.

6 Picture-Changing Patterns

1. **2.** 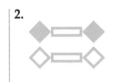 **3.** **4.** 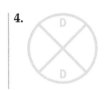 **5.** 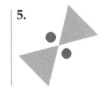 **6.**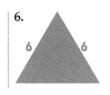

7 Spot the Metamorphosis!

1. 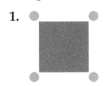 **2.**  **3.** 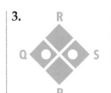 **4.** **5.**  **6.**

PATTERNS AT PLAY CONT'D

8 Marvelous Matrices

1.

2.

3.

9 It's Matrix Time!

1.

2.

```
O X X
X O O
O X X
```

10 Brain Bender

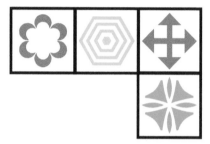

FOLLOW THAT ANALOGY

12 Shape Up Analogies

1.

2. 5

3.

4.

5.

6.

7.

8.

13 Sports Analogies

1. baseball
2. heavy
3. umpire
4. one
5. wheels
6. court
7. zero
8. soccer/hockey
9. water
10. small/little
11. pool
12. long

14 Yummy Analogies

1.

2.

3.

4.

5.

6.

7.

8.

FOLLOW THAT ANALOGY CONT'D

15 Animal Analogies

1. kitten
2. scales
3. dog
4. pack
5. slow
6. elephant
7. nest
8. jump/hop
9. lungs
10. spotted
11. fly
12. desert
13. slither
14. tiny/small
15. sly

16 Fractions and Letters Fun!

1. **L**

2.

3. **II**

4.

5. **KƆ**

6.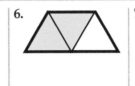

7. **M M M**

8.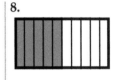

17 Analogies at Work!

1.

2.

3.

4.

5.

6.

7.

8. CHRIS HOW MAY I HELP YOU?

18 Mad About Math Analogies

1. divide
2. whole
3. midnight
4. 8
5. 10
6. length
7. 100
8. 360°
9. 144
10. 8
11. 9
12. 3D
13. triangles
14. 3, 5, 7, 9
15. 6

19 Analogies in the Mix!

1. porcupine/ hedgehog/ echidna
2. [map of United States]
3. yard
4. [cylinder]
5. [salamander]
6. tornado/ hurricane
7. 1 gallon
8. [circle divided with dots]

20 Brain Bender

1. C. snake : fangs
2. A. tedious : monotonous
3. C. furtive : tiptoe
4. B. salmon : fish
5. A. fascinating : boring
6. C. Paris : Eiffel Tower
7. B. content : ecstatic
8. C. writer : author
9. A. ebb : tide
10. B. stars : sailors

MISSION CODE BREAKERS

22 Morse Code Masterpieces

1. Mona Lisa   2. The Scream   3. Red Balloon   4. Composition VIII

23 I Scream, You Scream

Grid puzzle containing the words:
- BIRTHDAY
- ROCKYROAD
- MOCHA
- BANANA
- CHOCOLATE
- VANILLA
- CHERRY
- MINTCHIP
- BUBBLEGUM
- COOKIESANDCREAM

Cipher key:

1	2	3	4	5	6	7	8	9	10	11	12	13
M	O	C	H	A	Y	Z	W	D	P	E	S	F

14	15	16	17	18	19	20	21	22	23	24	25	26
K	Q	G	L	V	R	B	U	I	N	X	T	J

24 Binary Code Pictures

25 Fun and Games

Grid puzzle containing the words:
- CONNECT 4
- CLUE
- BINGO
- SORRY
- CHESS
- CHECKERS
- MONOPOLY
- TROUBLE
- LIFE
- SCRABBLE
- CANDYLAND
- MANCALA
- BATTLESHIP
- OPERATION

Cipher key:

1	2	3	4	5	6	7	8	9	10	11	12	13
L	I	F	E	P	K	W	B	H	U	J	Y	C

14	15	16	17	18	19	20	21	22	23	24	25	26
G	D	X	O	T	A	R	M	V	N	Z	S	Q

26 Pigpen

1. DOLPHINS
2. WARTHOGS
3. JET ENGINE
4. DENMARK

27 Outer Space

(crossword grid with answers: ECLIPSE, ASTRONAUT, SATURN, MARS, EARTH, ASTRONOMY, NEPTUNE, GALAXY, UNIVERSE, TELESCOPE, VENUS, SUN, MERCURY, TELESCOPE, COMET, etc.)

1	2	3	4	5	6	7	8	9	10	11	12	13
M	A	R	S	F	V	O	B	L	U	E	N	Y

14	15	16	17	18	19	20	21	22	23	24	25	26
P	G	K	I	C	Q	H	T	X	D	Z	J	W

28 Crack the Code

1. C. SA
2. A. LY
3. A. HD
4. C. FJ
5. D. LRS

29 Rainforest

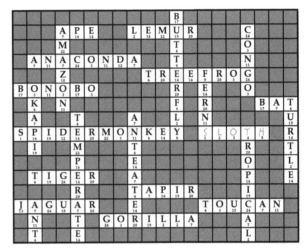

1	2	3	4	5	6	7	8	9	10	11	12	13
S	L	O	T	H	K	A	Y	F	W	N	D	J

14	15	16	17	18	19	20	21	22	23	24	25	26
E	U	P	B	Z	I	R	X	M	V	C	Q	G

30 Brain Bender

1. 7 4 8
2. 3 2 9
3. 5 6 1
4. 8 3 7

SIMPLY LOGICAL

32 Alien Landing

	AZENA	NOLP	ZEBLY	VAR
8	O	X	X	X
9	X	X	X	O
10	X	X	O	X
11	X	O	X	X

	AZENA	NOLP	ZEBLY	VAR
PANCAKES	X	X	O	X
JELLY BEANS	X	O	X	X
PICKLES	X	X	X	O
CORN DOGS	O	X	X	X

33 Picnic Time

	HOT DOGS	CHIPS	FRUIT	DRINKS
MICHAEL	X	O	X	X
MARIELA	X	X	O	X
JORDAN	O	X	X	X
RYAN	X	X	X	O

	DISTRACTION	CAMOUFLAGE	GRAB AND RUN	TIPTOE
ANTONIA	X	X	X	O
ANTERO	X	O	X	X
ANTOINETTE	X	X	O	X
ANTONELLO	O	X	X	X

34 At the Donut Shop

	WHOLE MILK	NONFAT MILK	ORANGE JUICE	HOT COCOA	GLAZED TWIST	JELLY FILLED	MAPLE BAR	APPLE FRITTER
JACKSON	X	X	O	X	X	O	X	X
MIA	X	O	X	X	X	X	O	X
ANDREW	O	X	X	X	O	X	X	X
LEE	X	X	X	O	X	X	X	O
GLAZED TWIST	O	X	X	X				
JELLY FILLED	X	X	O	X				
MAPLE BAR	X	O	X	X				
APPLE FRITTER	X	X	X	O				

35 Pirate Treasure

	SILVER TOOTH	MAD CAPTAIN	SHARP HOOK	JOLLY TWO TOES	GOLD	SILVER	JEWELS	GOLD COINS
MARIA	X	X	O	X	X	O	X	X
WILLIAM	X	O	X	X	O	X	X	X
ISABEL	O	X	X	X	X	X	O	X
CHARLES	X	X	X	O	X	X	X	O
GOLD	X	O	X	X				
SILVER	X	X	O	X				
JEWELS	O	X	X	X				
GOLD COINS	X	X	X	O				

36 Puppy Love

	PUG	BEAGLE	POODLE	COCKER SPANIEL	BORDER COLLIE	FRISBEE	CHEW TOY	TENNIS BALL	SQUEAKY PIZZA	BEAR
DAISY	X	O	X	X	X	X	O	X	X	X
ROCKY	X	X	X	O	O	X	X	O	X	X
SADIE	O	X	X	X	X	X	X	X	X	O
OLIVER	X	X	X	O	X	O	X	X	X	X
LOLA	X	X	O	X	X	X	X	X	O	X
FRISBEE	X	X	X	O	X					
CHEW TOY	X	O	X	X	X					
TENNIS BALL	X	X	X	X	O					
SQUEAKY PIZZA	X	X	O	X	X					
BEAR	O	X	X	X	X					

37 Museum Day

	BLACK	GRAY	GREEN	PURPLE	RED	MUMMY	T-REX FOSSIL	INSECTS	SHARK TEETH	AFRICAN SHIELDS
NICO	X	O	X	X	X	O	X	X	X	X
CLAIRE	X	X	O	X	X	X	X	X	O	X
BRAYTON	O	X	X	X	X	X	X	X	X	O
NALA	X	X	X	X	O	X	O	X	X	X
AIDEN	X	X	X	O	X	X	X	O	X	X
MUMMY	X	O	X	X	X					
T-REX FOSSIL	X	X	X	X	O					
INSECTS	X	X	X	O	X					
SHARK TEETH	X	X	O	X	X					
AFRICAN SHIELDS	O	X	X	X	X					

38 At the Carnival

	CORN DOGS	COTTON CANDY	FUNNEL CAKE	SOFT PRETZEL	SNOW CONE	MERRY-GO-ROUND	FERRIS WHEEL	BUMPER CARS	SWING RIDE	ROLLER COASTER
MARIANA	O	X	X	X	X	X	X	X	O	X
DANIEL	X	X	X	O	X	X	O	X	X	X
LUCIA	X	O	X	X	X	X	X	X	X	O
MATEO	X	X	O	X	X	O	X	X	X	X
JULIA	X	X	X	X	O	X	X	O	X	X
MERRY-GO-ROUND	X	X	O	X	X					
FERRIS WHEEL	X	X	X	O	X					
BUMPER CARS	X	X	X	X	O					
SWING RIDE	O	X	X	X	X					
ROLLER COASTER	X	O	X	X	X					

39 Tropical Fish

	$2.00	$4.00	$6.00	$8.00	$10.00	ANGELFISH	TIGER BARB	KOI	GOLDFISH	ZEBRA DANIO
JAKE	X	X	O	X	X	X	X	X	O	X
HANNA	X	O	X	X	X	X	O	X	X	X
DIEGO	X	X	X	O	X	O	X	X	X	X
OLIVIA	X	X	X	X	O	X	O	X	O	X
BEN	O	X	X	X	X	X	X	X	X	O
ANGELFISH	X	X	X	O	X					
TIGER BARB	X	O	X	X	X					
KOI	X	X	X	X	O					
GOLDFISH	X	X	O	X	X					
ZEBRA DANIO	O	X	X	X	X					

40 Brain Bender

	$2.00	$3.00	$4.00	$5.00	$8.00	RED	GOLD	SILVER	BLUE	GREEN	STAR	EMOJI	HAWK	SHARK	CAR
COURTNEY	X	X	X	X	O	X	O	X	X	X	O	X	X	X	X
ERIK	O	X	X	X	X	X	X	X	X	O	X	X	X	O	X
ROSE	X	X	X	O	X	X	X	X	O	X	X	X	X	X	O
ROBERT	X	O	X	X	X	X	O	X	X	X	X	X	O	X	X
COLLEEN	X	X	O	X	X	O	X	X	X	X	X	O	X	X	X
STAR	X	X	X	X	O	X	O	X	X	X					
EMOJI	X	X	O	X	X	O	X	X	X	X					
HAWK	X	O	X	X	X	X	X	O	X	X					
SHARK	O	X	X	X	X	X	X	X	X	O					
CAR	X	X	X	O	X	X	X	X	O	X					
RED	X	X	O	X	X										
GOLD	X	X	X	X	O										
SILVER	X	O	X	X	X										
BLUE	X	X	X	O	X										
GREEN	O	X	X	X	X										

CROSSWORDS TO CONSIDER

42 Where in the World?

43 Coral Reef

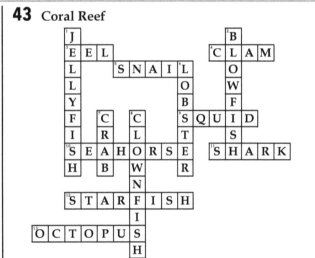

44 It's About Time

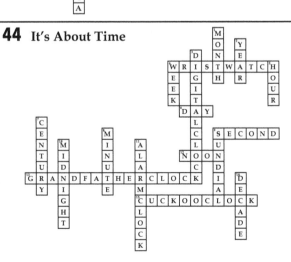

45 Fruity Fun

CROSSWORDS TO CONSIDER CONT'D

46 Desert Animals

47 What's the Weather?

48 Once Upon a Time

49 Geology

50 Brain Bender

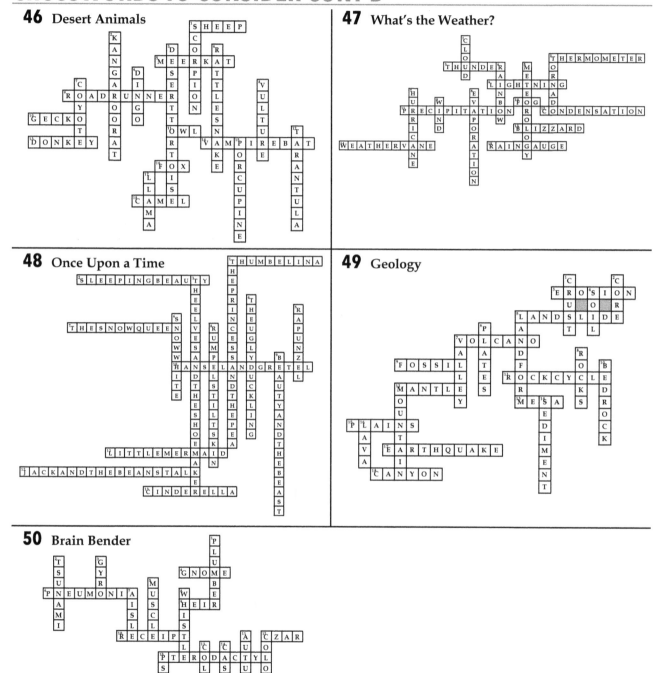

WHIMSICAL WORDS

52 Dee-lish
1. pig in a blanket
2. cookies and milk
3. scrambled eggs
4. orange marmalade
5. banana split
6. pumpkin pie

53 It's a Zoo in Here!
1. little fish in a big pond
2. monkey around
3. the top dog
4. nine lives
5. a fat cat
6. a red herring (A clue meant to distract you)

54 Back to Nature
1. once in a blue moon
2. a line in the sand
3. up in the air
4. a storm in a teacup
5. a half moon
6. second nature

55 Let's Go!
1. big wheel
2. crossroads
3. broken down
4. two-way street
5. putting the cart before the horse
6. four-wheeler

56 Human Body
1. splitting hairs
2. tongue in cheek
3. thumbs up
4. head over heels
5. right under your nose
6. five senses

57 Cool School!
1. learn by heart
2. pass with flying colors
3. count noses
4. reading books back to back
5. one-on-one help
6. left brain and right brain

58 Idioms
1. once bitten twice shy
2. double-cross
3. two peas in a pod
4. six of one, half a dozen of the other
5. the last straw
6. between life and death

59 Get to Work
1. all in a day's work
2. keep your head above water
3. a balance of power
4. work around the clock
5. think outside the box
6. split decisions

60 Brain Bender
1. cut corners
2. down to the wire
3. a gray area
4. a bull in a china shop
5. lickety split
6. turn upside down
7. two left feet
8. walking in circles
9. hot under the collar

MINDFUL MATH

62 Sudoku: Llama

4	2	3	1
3	1	2	4
1	3	4	2
2	4	1	3

1	2	4	3
3	4	2	1
4	3	1	2
2	1	3	4

2	1	4	3
4	3	1	2
1	2	3	4
3	4	2	1

4	3	2	1
1	2	3	4
2	4	1	3
3	1	4	2

63 Mathdoku: Yo-Yo

24x 2	3	4 4	3+ 1
4	4+ 1	3	2
8+ 3	2 2	3- 1	4
1	4	5+ 2	3

9+ 2	4	2- 1	3
12x 4	3	7+ 2	1 1
1	2	3	8x 4
3	4+ 1	4	2

24x 2	4	3	1 1
1 1	2	2- 4	5+ 3
8+ 4	3	1	2
4+ 3	1	6+ 2	4

1- 1	6+ 2	4	3 3
2	2- 1	7+ 3	4
11+ 4	3	4+ 2	1
3	4	1	2 2

MINDFUL MATH CONT'D

64 Sudoku: Panda and Baby

6	1	5	4	3	2
3	4	2	5	6	1
2	6	1	3	4	5
5	3	4	2	1	6
1	2	3	6	5	4
4	5	6	1	2	3

3	2	1	4
4	1	3	2
1	4	2	3
2	3	4	1

65 Mathdoku: Spinning Tops

4	2	5	1	6	3
1	6	3	5	4	2
2	4	1	6	3	5
3	5	2	4	1	6
6	3	4	2	5	1
5	1	6	3	2	4

2	4	1	3
4	1	3	2
3	2	4	1
1	3	2	4

66 Sudoku: Giraffe

1	8	3	2	4	7	6	5
6	4	7	5	1	8	3	2
2	6	4	3	7	1	5	8
5	1	8	7	2	6	4	3
4	7	5	1	8	3	2	6
3	2	6	8	5	4	7	1
7	5	1	6	3	2	8	4
8	3	2	4	6	5	1	7

67 Mathdoku: Boomerang

4	8	3	2	6	7	1	5
2	6	1	7	5	4	8	3
7	3	8	1	2	5	4	6
6	2	5	3	8	1	7	4
8	1	2	4	3	6	5	7
1	5	7	6	4	2	3	8
3	4	6	5	7	8	2	1
5	7	4	8	1	3	6	2

68 Sudoku: Kangaroo

4	3	9	1	8	5	2	6	7
8	1	2	6	9	7	4	3	5
6	7	5	3	2	4	1	8	9
1	9	3	2	5	8	6	7	4
5	2	4	9	7	6	8	1	3
7	6	8	4	1	3	5	9	2
2	5	1	8	3	9	7	4	6
3	4	7	5	6	1	9	2	8
9	8	6	7	4	2	3	5	1

69 Mathdoku: Robot

3	9	2	4	7	5	8	6	1
4	8	1	6	5	2	9	3	7
7	3	6	5	2	9	1	4	8
8	7	3	2	4	1	6	5	9
9	2	8	1	3	6	4	7	5
1	6	5	8	9	4	7	2	3
2	1	4	3	8	7	5	9	6
6	5	7	9	1	3	2	8	4
5	4	9	7	6	8	3	1	2

70 Brain Bender

3	7	5	9	2	4	1	8	6
6	4	8	1	3	5	9	2	7
2	1	9	6	7	8	4	5	3
1	5	6	2	9	3	7	4	8
4	8	3	5	1	7	2	6	9
9	2	7	4	8	6	3	1	5
8	3	4	7	6	2	5	9	1
5	6	1	3	4	9	8	7	2
7	9	2	8	5	1	6	3	4

CURI_US CRYPT_GRAMS

72 Basketball Facts

A	B	C	D	E	F	G	H	I	J	K	L	M	N	O	P	Q	R	S	T	U	V	W	X	Y	Z
7	1	14	20	8	2	15	9	21	16	3	10	22	17	23	4	18	12	24	5	19	25	13	6	26	

BASKETBALL WAS INVENTED
1 7 12 3 8 24 1 7 10 10 25 7 12 21 17 19 8 17 24 8 20

DURING WINTER AS AN
20 5 18 21 17 15 25 21 17 24 8 18 7 12 7 17

INDOOR GAME.
21 17 20 11 11 18 15 7 22 8

A	B	C	D	E	F	G	H	I	J	K	L	M	N	O	P	Q	R	S	T	U	V	W	X	Y	Z
5	8	6	16	4	12	7	23	3	10	14	21	11	13	25	2	15	1	19	9	24	17	26	18	20	22

PEACH BASKETS WERE USED
2 4 5 6 23 8 5 19 14 4 9 19 26 4 1 4 24 19 4 16

AS THE FIRST BASKETBALL
5 19 9 23 4 12 3 1 19 9 8 5 19 14 4 9 8 5 21 21

HOOPS.
23 25 25 2 19

73 Aesop's Fables

A	B	C	D	E	F	G	H	I	J	K	L	M	N	O	P	Q	R	S	T	U	V	W	X	Y	Z
10	16	24	2	9	17	23	1	8	11	3	18	12	4	25	22	13	21	14	5	20	7	15	26	6	19

DON'T COUNT YOUR
2 25 4 5   24 25 20 4 5   6 25 20 21

CHICKENS UNTIL
24 1 8 24 3 9 4 14   20 4 5 8 18

THEY'RE HATCHED.
5 1 9 6 21 9   1 10 5 24 1 9 2

A	B	C	D	E	F	G	H	I	J	K	L	M	N	O	P	Q	R	S	T	U	V	W	X	Y	Z
7	8	6	17	25	5	21	9	18	10	15	20	3	11	26	19	12	2	13	14	23	22	1	24	16	4

WHATEVER YOU DO,
1 9 7 14 25 22 25 2   16 26 23   17 26

DO WITH ALL YOUR
17 26   1 18 14 9   7 20 20   16 26 23 2

MIGHT.
3 18 21 2 14

74 Castles

A	B	C	D	E	F	G	H	I	J	K	L	M	N	O	P	Q	R	S	T	U	V	W	X	Y	Z
6	15	1	24	7	23	14	2	22	8	13	21	3	9	12	18	20	4	5	11	10	25	16	17	19	26

THE FIRST CASTLES WERE
11 2 7   23 22 4 5 11   1 6 5 11 21 7 5   16 7 4 7

BUILT OF WOOD, BUT LATER
15 10 22 21 11   12 23   16 12 12 24   15 10 11   21 6 11 7 4

THEY USED STONE.
11 2 7 19   10 5 7 24   5 11 12 9 7

A	B	C	D	E	F	G	H	I	J	K	L	M	N	O	P	Q	R	S	T	U	V	W	X	Y	Z
2	6	12	18	5	4	11	17	10	19	13	8	16	20	1	25	15	21	3	7	22	26	23	24	9	14

CASTLES WERE OFTEN BUILT
12 2 3 7 8 5 3   23 5 21 5   1 4 7 5 20   6 22 10 8 7

ON THE TOP OF A HILL.
1 20   7 17 5   7 1 25   1 4   2   17 10 8 8

75 Dolphins

A	B	C	D	E	F	G	H	I	J	K	L	M	N	O	P	Q	R	S	T	U	V	W	X	Y	Z
4	12	3	5	2	26	10	14	6	13	16	8	19	9	7	15	20	21	1	22	25	11	17	24	18	23

A DOLPHIN EATS ABOUT
4   5 7 8 15 14 6 9   2 4 22 1   4 12 7 25 22

THIRTY POUNDS OF FISH
22 14 6 21 22 18   15 7 25 9 5 1   7 26   26 6 1 14

EACH DAY.
2 4 3 14   5 4 18

A	B	C	D	E	F	G	H	I	J	K	L	M	N	O	P	Q	R	S	T	U	V	W	X	Y	Z
9	18	10	3	1	25	17	2	8	24	12	11	16	21	4	22	23	15	5	14	6	20	7	26	13	19

DOLPHINS ARE SOCIAL
3 4 11 22 2 8 21 5   9 15 1   5 4 10 8 9 11

ANIMALS, SO THEY LIVE AND
9 21 8 16 9 11 5   5 4   14 2 1 13   11 8 20 1   9 21 3

HUNT IN GROUPS.
2 6 21 14   8 21   17 15 4 6 22 5

76 Eiffel Tower

A	B	C	D	E	F	G	H	I	J	K	L	M	N	O	P	Q	R	S	T	U	V	W	X	Y	Z
7	6	20	5	19	1	21	8	9	14	22	2	13	26	3	23	18	12	4	11	17	25	10	24	16	15

MORE THAN SEVEN MILLION
13 3 12 19   11 8 7 26   4 19 25 19 26   13 9 2 2 9 3 26

PEOPLE VISIT THIS FAMOUS
23 19 3 23 2 19   25 9 4 9 11   11 8 9 4   1 7 13 3 17 4

MONUMENT EACH YEAR.
13 3 26 17 13 19 26 11   19 7 20 8   16 19 7 12

A	B	C	D	E	F	G	H	I	J	K	L	M	N	O	P	Q	R	S	T	U	V	W	X	Y	Z
3	4	6	9	17	5	11	18	10	19	7	20	16	21	2	15	22	25	1	26	23	8	12	24	13	14

IT TOOK THREE HUNDRED
10 26   26 2 2 7   26 18 25 17 17   18 23 21 9 25 17 9

WORKERS ABOUT TWO YEARS
12 2 25 7 17 25 1   3 4 2 23 26   26 12 2   13 17 3 25 1

TO BUILD THE EIFFEL TOWER.
26 2   4 23 10 20 9   26 18 17   17 10 5 5 17 20   26 2 12 17 25

111

77 Volcanoes

A	B	C	D	E	F	G	H	I	J	K	L	M	N	O	P	Q	R	S	T	U	V	W	X	Y	Z
7	23	14	5	11	26	15	6	10	18	16	1	9	22	24	2	17	25	3	19	12	20	8	13	4

ERUPTIONS CAN SEND ASH
11 21 19 2 3 10 24 22 25   14 7 22   25 11 22 5   7 25 6

OVER SEVENTEEN MILES IN
24 12 11 21   25 11 12 11 22 3 11 11 22   9 10 1 11 25   10 22

THE AIR.
3 6 11   7 10 21

A	B	C	D	E	F	G	H	I	J	K	L	M	N	O	P	Q	R	S	T	U	V	W	X	Y	Z
8	16	5	22	4	25	15	3	9	17	19	10	14	18	1	24	11	2	13	21	7	20	6	23	12	26

MOST OF THE WORLD'S BIGGEST
14 1 13 21   1 25   21 3 4   6 1 2 10 22 13   16 9 15 15 4 13 21

ERUPTIONS HAPPEN IN
4 2 7 24 21 9 1 18 13   3 8 24 24 4 18   9 18

THE PACIFIC RING OF FIRE.
21 3 4   24 8 5 9 25 9 5   2 9 18 15   1 25   25 9 2 4

78 Pizza

A	B	C	D	E	F	G	H	I	J	K	L	M	N	O	P	Q	R	S	T	U	V	W	X	Y	Z
7	12	8	21	1	20	22	9	10	13	11	2	26	18	19	3	25	14	4	15	17	5	16	24	23	6

OVER FIVE BILLION PIZZAS
19 5 1 14   20 10 5 1   12 10 2 2 10 19 18   3 10 6 6 7 4

ARE SOLD WORLDWIDE EACH
7 14 1   4 19 2 21   16 19 14 2 21 16 10 21 1   1 7 8 9

YEAR.
23 1 7 14

A	B	C	D	E	F	G	H	I	J	K	L	M	N	O	P	Q	R	S	T	U	V	W	X	Y	Z
4	12	24	6	5	20	7	13	8	19	14	9	18	2	22	1	21	10	15	11	17	23	16	25	26	3

THE MOST POPULAR PIZZA
11 13 5   18 22 15 11   1 22 1 17 9 4 10   1 8 3 3 4

DELIVERY DAYS ARE HALLOWEEN
6 5 9 8 23 5 10 26   6 4 26 15   4 10 5   13 4 9 9 22 16 5 5 2

AND SUPER BOWL SUNDAY.
4 2 6   15 17 1 5 10   12 22 16 9   15 17 2 6 4 26

79 Mount Everest

A	B	C	D	E	F	G	H	I	J	K	L	M	N	O	P	Q	R	S	T	U	V	W	X	Y	Z
5	11	21	2	20	10	19	1	12	18	22	3	9	6	13	17	16	26	4	24	14	7	25	15	8	23

MORE THAN FOUR THOUSAND
9 13 26 20   24 1 5 6   10 13 14 26   24 1 13 14 4 5 6 2

HAVE SUCCESSFULLY CLIMBED
1 5 7 20   4 14 21 21 20 4 10 14 3 3 8   21 3 12 9 11 20 2

TO THE TOP OF THE MOUNTAIN.
24 13   24 1 20   24 13 17   13 10   24 1 20   9 13 14 6 24 5 12 6

A	B	C	D	E	F	G	H	I	J	K	L	M	N	O	P	Q	R	S	T	U	V	W	X	Y	Z
6	11	7	17	8	16	10	22	1	15	23	2	12	3	18	4	25	19	21	5	24	13	9	20	14	26

FROM THE SUMMIT, YOU CAN
16 19 18 12   5 22 8   21 24 12 12 1 5   14 18 24   7 6 3

SEE TIBET, INDIA, AND
21 8 8   5 1 11 8 5   1 3 17 1 6   6 3 17

NEPAL.
3 8 4 6 2

80 Brain Bender

A	B	C	D	E	F	G	H	I	J	K	L	M	N	O	P	Q	R	S	T	U	V	W	X	Y	Z
7	5	17	15	1	18	26	6	10	24	25	14	2	22	8	12	23	9	13	16	3	19	11	20	4	21

WASHING MACHINE CAR
11 7 13 6 10 22 26   2 7 17 6 10 22 1   17 7 9

TELEPHONE PAPER WHEEL
16 1 14 1 12 6 8 22 1   12 7 12 1 9   11 6 1 1 14

PRINTING PRESS COMPASS
12 9 10 22 16 10 22 26   12 9 1 13 13   17 8 2 12 7 13 13

LIGHTBULB COMPUTER
14 10 26 6 16 5 3 14 5   17 8 2 12 3 16 1 9

AIRPLANE TELESCOPE
7 10 9 12 14 7 22 1   16 1 14 1 13 17 8 12 1

AIR CONDITIONING PEN
7 10 9   17 8 22 15 10 16 10 8 22 10 22 26   12 1 22

112

MIND YOUR MATCHSTICKS

82 Something's Fishy

1.

2.

3.

83 Eagle Eyes!

1.

Or

2.

3.

84 A Square Deal

1.

 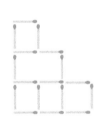

2. Rectangles are: ABKJ, CDML, EFON, GHQP, AFOJ, CHQL, AHQL. Squares are: ADMJ, CFOL, EHQN

 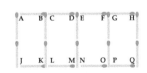

3.

 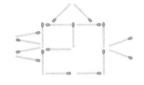

85 Number Sleuth

1.

2.

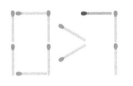 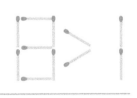

3.

 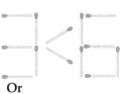

Or

MIND YOUR MATCHSTICKS CONT'D

86 Try It Triangles!

1.

2.

3.

87 Whooo Can Solve These?

1.

2.

Or

3.

 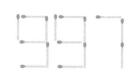

88 Back to Square One!

1.

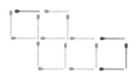

2.

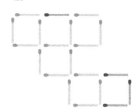 

3.

 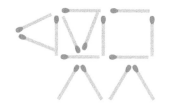

89 Number Scramble

1.

2.

3.

90 Brain Bender

How many squares are there? 50

ODD BIRDS

92 Shaping Up!

1. D

2. C

3. C

4. B

93 A Dozen Differences

1. VYZ
2. 357
3. Crater

4. Dollar
5. .75
6. Thrilled

7. Rake
8. Trumpet
9. 336

10. 543
11. Sand
12. Clarinet

94 Seeing Spots!

1. C

2. E

3. C

4. A

95 Which One Is Different?

1. Robin
2. Fractions
3. 45

4. Crust
5. 5/4
6. Ounce

7. Pizza pan
8. Sculpture
9. 11

10. B
11. Shirt
12. Asia

96 Fair and Square

1. A

2. C

3. D

4. E

ODD BIRDS CONT'D

97 Oddballs

1. Red fox
2. Feet
3. 7
4. Beethoven
5. 3/7
6. Rain
7. Mexico
8. Piano
9. 3.5
10. X
11. Badminton
12. Mountain

98 All Lined Up!

1. C

2. D

3. E

4. B

99 Square Pegs

1. Salamander
2. Trapezoid
3. 16 oz. = 2 lb.
4. Steel
5. Buddhism
6. Spider
7. Fern
8. Matisse
9. 789
10. Forty-fives
11. Tower of Pisa
12. Neutron star

100 Brain Bender

First Row

2.

Second Row

1. Mint
2. Accountant
3. Blouse
4. Attempt
5. Screwdriver

Third Row

2.

8	N	$
&	A	4
V	#	M

Fourth Row

1. 11
2. Mouse = 15
3. 25 dollars
4. 26
5. 45317

ACKNOWLEDGMENTS

A million thanks to everyone at Callisto Media who worked so hard to make this book a reality. I am especially grateful for my amazing editor, Lia Brown. Her insightful ideas and her guidance were invaluable.

I am so grateful for my daughter, Courtney Larson, who was my second set of eyes. She read each chapter and solved each puzzle along the way. Her constant encouragement meant everything.

My son, Erik Larson, and his wife, Colleen Larson, also have my appreciation. Their enthusiasm for this project and their support uplifts me, and I am so thankful for them.

For all the ways he's believed in me, pushed me, and cheered me on, I am so thankful for my boyfriend, Richard Carvalho. He continually tells me how proud of me he is, and he never stops believing in me.

My parents have both passed away but they are always close in my heart. I am forever indebted to them. For my father, Robert Schmoll, who taught me to have a strong work ethic, to look for humor wherever you can, and to find joy in creativity, I am truly thankful.

For my mother, Rose Schmoll, who taught me fierce determination, to follow your dreams, and to have a caring heart, I am so very grateful.

Finally, I am very appreciative of all the great teachers who sparked a sense of curiosity in me and who made learning fun. Mrs. Thoman, Ms. Plumlee, Mr. McCutcheon, Mr. Hefner, Mrs. Hofstedder, and Mr. Carson in particular have been an inspiration to me, and I will never forget any of them.

ABOUT THE AUTHOR

Jenn Larson graduated with a degree in Psychology but fell in love with teaching when she worked as a substitute teacher. She went back to college and earned her teaching credential and a Master's degree in Curriculum and Instruction.

Jenn has taught elementary students for over 20 years. Most of that time has been spent working with second, fourth, and fifth graders. Her philosophy of building strong relationships with students, creating a positive classroom climate, and making learning fun is a guiding influence on everything she does.

In addition to teaching, Jenn is the owner of The Teacher Next Door. She writes blog posts to share teaching activities and ideas with classroom teachers and homeschool parents. She also creates teaching resources on Teachers Pay Teachers that are not only time-saving for teachers, but also provide standards-based activities that students enjoy.

Family is important to Jenn and she has two kids, Erik (an analyst in the video game industry) and Courtney (a college student and future teacher), as well as a daughter-in-law, Colleen (an artist in the video game industry), and a boyfriend, Richard (a retired firefighter). She also has three rescue cats.

Jenn loves movies, spending time in nature (but sleeping in a hotel), snow skiing, and anything slightly daring, like zip lining and rappelling off bridges or into caverns.

To connect with Jenn, you can find her as The Teacher Next Door on Facebook, Instagram, Twitter, Pinterest, and her website (www.The-Teacher-Next-Door.com).